The Air Fryer Bible

*Complete Cookbook of Super Easy
Recipes for Everyday Meals*

Linda Shaw

Additionally, the information found on the following pages is intended for informational purposes only and should thus be considered, universal. As befitting its nature, the information presented is without assurance regarding its continued validity or interim quality. Trademarks that mentioned are done without written consent and can in no way be considered an endorsement from the trademark holder.

Table of Contents

Introduction

I am so glad you took the time to download your copy of *The Air Fryer Bible: Complete Cookbook of Super Easy Recipes for Everyday Meals* with over 150 healthy choices. Thank you for doing so. Hot air frying is a cooking method that allows grilling, steaming, frying, and roasting without the use of large amounts of oil. You enjoy that deep-fried taste and texture without the overuse of oil.

Several types are on the market dating back to the commercial basket hot air fryer invented in 1999, the paddle-type Actifry unit in 2006, and lastly - the domestic basket hot air fryer designed in 2010 with the improved Philips Air Fryer. Just when you believed there was no alternative, and fried foods were barred from your life forever, you can now enjoy your favorite fried foods as a part of your daily diet.

You can experiment with more types of oil including coconut oil, grapeseed oil, walnut oil, and avocado oil. These are healthier oils, which make the sky the limit for tasty fried foods you can now enjoy with your new Air Fryer. Low-fat air fryer cooking will provide you with foods prepared with the circulation of hot air. All of the excess fat can drip down into a tray below the cooking basket. The compact air fryer allows you to set the cooking temperature and timer. All you need to do is - wait for the beep, and your food is ready for the table.

You will not need to a have a messy workspace, since there is not much to clean. Cooking food in the fryer is fast, safe, and healthy – any time- day or night.

One Quick Tip Before You Begin: You might need to use a sling when lowering a pan into the air fryer. Fold a section of aluminum foil into a strip into lengths long enough to fit under the pan, and not be burned in the process. It should be cut into pieces of 2x24-inches.

The following chapters will discuss some of the many different ways you can stay in tune with your health using your Air Fryer. There are plenty of books offered on this subject in today's market, thanks again for choosing this one! Every effort was made to ensure that it is full of as much useful information as possible.

Please enjoy!

If you like this book, please let us know by leaving us a review.

Now Let's begin...

Chapter 1: The Air Fryer Benefits & User Tips

Benefits over Traditional Frying Methods

Benefit 1: It is perfect for a beginner. You can locate your favorite recipes and prepare an extraordinary meal at home in half of the time. The machine does the hard work for you. All you need to do is plug-in in the temperature and times.

Benefit 2: The Air Fryer will use much less oil. It won't be necessary to add a lot of oil to the cooker if you have frozen products which are meant for baking. You only need to adjust the timer and cook. All of the excess fat will drip away into a tray beneath the basket.

You can cook whatever meats you enjoy and receive delicious and healthy results. You will understand this once you begin trying out some of these new recipes.
For example, you can cook French fries with a tablespoon of oil versus a vat of oil.

Benefit 3: Purchase a high-quality oil. It is possible to splurge on the more expensive oils since you only use such a minimal amount.

Benefit 4: No messy oils to clean. You only need to remove the cooking bowl, drip pan, or the cooking basket. It is inside a cover, which means you will not have oil vapor deposits on the walls, floors, or countertops. You can use the dishwasher to clean the movable parts. You can also use a sponge to clean the bits of food that might be stuck to the AF surfaces.

Benefit 5: The fryer has many functional uses. The Air Fryer is capable of functioning as so many products, whether you need an oven, a hot grill, a toaster, a skillet, or a deep fryer—the unit is your answer! It can be used for breakfast, lunch, dinner, desserts, and even snacks.

Benefit 6: You are provided with many safety functions. The machine will automatically shut down when the cooking time is completed. You will have less burned or overheated food items. The fryer will not slip because of the non-slip feet that help eliminate the risk of the machine from falling off the countertop. The closed cooking system helps prevent burns from hot oil or other foods.

Tips for Using the Air Fryer

Tip 1: It is tempting when you are in a rush to attempt to overload the Air Fryer. You don't want to put too much in the cooking basket at one time. You won't receive the best results if the air cannot make the 360° turns that make the cooker so unique.

Tip 2: Cooking sprays are an excellent choice to spray on your food before cooking. You can also spray the mesh of the cooking basket to keep anything from sticking to its surface.

Tip 3: Many pre-made packaged food items can be cooked using the Air Fryer. Each food may vary with its cooking time. As a rule-of-thumb, reduce the cooking times by about 70% compared to times in a conventional oven.

Tip 4: While cooking smaller items such as fries or wings; you can make sure they are cooking evenly by shaking the basket several times during the cooking process.

Tip 5: It is imperative to pat food items dry if you have marinated or soaked them in to help eliminate splattering or excessive smoke.

Tip 6: Allow at least three minutes of warm-up time each time you use the fryer so it can reach its correct starting temperature.

Tip 7: If you use aluminum foil or parchment paper, leave a one-half-inch space around the bottom edge of the basket.

Tip 8: When it comes time to clean the cooking basket, loosen any food particles remaining attached to the basket. Soak each of the attachments in a soapy water solution before scrubbing or placing it in the dishwasher.

Now, it is time to enjoy using your Air Fryer with each of the following chapters of tasty and easily prepared dishes.

Chapter 2: Breakfast & Brunch Recipes

Whether you choose the basic eggs or a delicious sweet treat, you will find the cure in this segment!

Air Bread with Egg Butter

Yields: 19 Servings

Ingredients for the Air Bread:

3 eggs
1 t. baking powder
1 c. almond flour
¼ t. sea salt
¼ c. butter

How to Prepare the Bread:

1. Soften the butter to room temperature. Whisk the eggs with a hand mixer. Combine the two and add the rest of the fixings to make a dough.
2. Knead the dough and cover with a tea towel for about 10 minutes.
3. Set the Air Fryer at 350°F.
4. Air fry the bread 15 minutes. Check the center with a toothpick for doneness.
5. Remove the bread and let it cool down on a wooden board.
6. Slice and serve with your favorite meal or as it is.

Egg Butter

Yields: 4 Servings

Ingredients for the Egg Butter:

4 eggs
1 t. salt
4 tbsp. butter

How to Prepare:

1. Add a layer of foil to the Air Fryer basket and add the eggs. Cook at 320°F for 17 minutes. Transfer to an ice-cold water bath to chill.
2. Peel and chop the eggs and combine with the rest of the fixings. Mix well until it reaches a creamy texture.
3. Enjoy with your Air Fried Bread.

Apple Dumplings

Yields: 2 Servings

Ingredients:

2 tbsp. raisins
2 small apples
1 tbsp. brown sugar
2 sheets puff pastry
2 tbsp. melted butter

How to Prepare:

1. Peel and core the apples.
2. Warm up the Air Fryer to 356°F.
3. Mix the sugar and raisins. Arrange each apple on one of the pastry sheets and fill with the raisins/sugar.
4. Fold the pastry over until the apple and raisins are adequately covered. Place them on a piece of foil so they cannot fall through the fryer. Thoroughly brush them with the melted butter.
5. Air fry for 25 minutes until they are golden browned.

Suggestion: Be sure to use tiny apples for this yummy treat.

Avocado Egg Boats

Yields: 2 Servings

Ingredients:

1 avocado
2 large eggs
To Taste:
 -Freshly chopped chives and parsley
 -Pepper
 -Salt

How to Prepare:

1. Warm up the fryer to 350°F.
2. Remove the pit from the avocado and remove some of the flesh. Shake with the seasonings.
3. Add an egg to each half and place in the preheated Air Fryer for 6 minutes.
4. Remove and serve with some additional parsley and chives if desired.

Avocado Muffins

Yields: 7 Servings

Ingredients:

1 c. almond flour
½ t. baking soda
1 t. apple cider vinegar
1 egg
4 tbsp. butter
3 scoops of stevia powder
½ c. pitted avocado
1 oz. melted dark chocolate

How to Prepare:

1. Preheat the Air Fryer to 355°F.
2. Whisk the vinegar with the baking soda and almond flour. Add the stevia powder and melted chocolate.
3. Whisk the egg in another container and add to the mixture along with the butter.
4. Peel, cube, and mash the avocado and add. Blend with a hand mixer to make the flour mixture smooth. Pour into the muffin forms (½ full). Cook for 9 minutes.
5. Lower the heat (340°F) and cook 3 more minutes.
6. Chill before serving for the best results.

Bacon & Cheese Muffins

Yields: 6 Servings

Ingredients:

1 large egg
4 large slices of bacon
1 med. diced onion
2 tbsp. olive oil
2 t. baking powder
1 c. of each:
-Milk
-Shredded cheddar cheese
1 ½ c. almond flour
1 t. parsley
Pepper and salt to taste

Also Needed: 6 muffin tins to fit in the basket

How to Prepare:

1. Set the temperature on the Air Fryer to 356°F.
2. Prepare the bacon slices with a small amount of oil. Add the onion when it's about ¾ ready. Sauté and set aside when translucent. Drain on towels.
3. Mix the rest of the fixings and stir well. Add the onions and bacon.
4. Stir well and add the batter into 6 muffin holders. Add to the fryer basket for 20 minutes. Lower the heat for 10 minutes (320°F).
5. Serve and enjoy right out of the fryer.

Bacon and Eggs

Ingredients:

4 eggs
12 (1/2-inch thick) slices of bacon
Pepper and salt
1 tbsp. butter
2 sliced croissants
4 tbsp. softened butter

BBQ Sauce Ingredients:

¼ c. apple cider vinegar
2 tbsp. each:
-Molasses
-Brown sugar
1 c. ketchup
½ t. each:
-Onion powder
-Mustard powder
- Liquid smoke
1 tbsp. Worcestershire sauce

How to Prepare:

1. Preheat the temperature in the Air Fryer to 390°F.
2. On the stovetop, using medium heat—mix the molasses, ketchup, brown sugar, vinegar, onion powder, and mustard powder using a small saucepot. Whisk the liquid smoke and Worcestershire sauce into the mixture to blend thoroughly. Cook until the sauce thickens. Add additional flavoring as desired.

3. Arrange the bacon on the trays and cook for five minutes. Remove and brush the bacon with the barbecue sauce –flip—and brush the other side—return to the cooker and continue cooking another five minutes.

4. Butter the halved croissant and toast it in the fryer.

5. In the meantime, use a non-stick pan on the med-low setting on the stovetop to melt the butter. Add four eggs to the pan, cooking until the white starts setting. Flip and cook about thirty more seconds.

6. Remove from the pan and enjoy with the bacon and croissant.

Baked Eggs in a Bread Bowl

Yields: 4 Egg Bowls

Ingredients:

4 large eggs
4 dinner rolls – crusty
4 tbsp. of each:
-Heavy cream
-Mixed herbs – for ex. Chopped tarragon, chives, parsley, etc.
-Grated parmesan cheese

How to Prepare:

1. Program the Air Fryer to 350°F.
2. Use a sharp knife to remove the top of each of the rolls – setting them aside for later. Scoop out some of the bread to form a hole large enough for the egg.
3. Place the rolls in the fryer basket. Break an egg into the roll and top with the cream and herbs. Sprinkle with some parmesan.
4. Bake for about 20-25 minutes until the egg is set. The bread should be toasted.
5. After 20 minutes, arrange the tops of the bread on the egg and bake a few more minutes to finish the browning process.
6. Let the eggs rest for five minutes. Serve warm.

Banana Fritters

Ingredients:

8 ripe peeled bananas
3 tbsp. corn flour
1 egg white
3 tbsp. vegetable oil
¾ c. breadcrumbs

How to Prepare:

1. Program the fryer to 356°F.
2. In a skillet using the low heat setting, pour the oil and toss in the breadcrumbs, cooking until golden brown.
3. Use the flour to coat the bananas. Dip them into the egg white, and cover with the breadcrumbs.
4. Place the bananas in a single layer of the basket and air fry for eight minutes.
5. Remove and sit on paper towels.

Breakfast Burrito

Yields: 1-2 Servings

Ingredients:

2 eggs
3-4 slices chicken or turkey breast
¼ sliced of each:
-Avocado
-Bell pepper
1/8 c. mozzarella cheese – grated
Pinch of pepper and salt
2 tbsp. salsa
1 tortilla

How to Prepare:

1. In a small mixing dish, whisk the eggs, and add salt and pepper to your liking.
2. Add the mixture into a small pan/tin and arrange it in the AF basket.
3. Cook for five minutes at 392°F.
4. When done, transfer the egg from the pan and fill the tortilla. Combine all of the ingredients and wrap it, but do not over-stuff.
5. Add a piece of foil to the Air Fryer tray and add the burrito. Heat for three minutes at 356°F.
6. The cheese will be melted and the tortilla crispy. Garnish as desired and enjoy!

Cheesy Ham – Egg & Mushroom

Yields: 1 Serving

Ingredients:

3 slices honey shaved ham
1 croissant
4 halved cherry tomatoes
4 small quartered button mushrooms
1 egg
1.8 oz. mozzarella or cheddar cheese
Optional: ½ roughly chopped rosemary sprig

How to Prepare:

1. Lightly grease a baking dish with butter to prevent the mixture from sticking.
2. Set the temperature in advance for the Air Fryer to 320°F.
3. Arrange the ingredients on two layers of cheese in the center and top layer.
4. Make a space in the center of the ham and crack the egg.
5. Sprinkle the rosemary and a smidgen of salt and pepper for flavoring over the mixture.
6. Put it into the preheated basket for eight minutes. Take the croissant out of the fryer after four minutes to allow more time for the egg to cook.
7. Serve when it is done to your liking.

Egg Cups & Bacon

Yields: 4 Servings

Ingredients:

4 eggs
½ t. of each:
 -Dried dill
 -Paprika
¼ t. salt
6 oz. bacon
1 tbsp. butter

Also Needed: 4 ramekins

How to Prepare:

1. Preheat the Air Fryer to 360°F.
2. Whisk the eggs and add the salt, paprika, and dried dill (a hand mixer is faster).
3. Coat the ramekins with butter. Slice the bacon and add to the cups.
4. Pour the egg fixings into the centers and air fry for 15 minutes.
5. Gently remove the cups and serve.

Egg Pizza

Yields: 1 Serving

Ingredients:

2 eggs
½ t. dried of each:
 -Oregano
 -Basil
2 tbsp. shredded mozzarella cheese
4 thin slices of pepperoni

Also Needed: 1 ramekin

How to Prepare:

1. Whisk the eggs with the oregano and basil.
2. Pour into the ramekin and top off with the pepperoni and cheese.
3. Arrange the ramekin in the air fryer. Prepare for 3 minutes and serve.

Eggs, Ham & Spinach

Yields: 4 Servings

Ingredients:

7 oz. sliced ham
2 ¼ c. spinach
4 t. cream milk
1 tbsp. olive oil
4 large eggs
To Taste: Salt and pepper

Also Needed:

4 ramekins
Cooking spray
1 Skillet

How to Prepare:

1. Set the fryer temperature to 356°F. Spray the ramekins.
2. Warm up the oil in a skillet (med. heat) and sauté the spinach until wilted. Drain.
3. Divide the spinach and the rest of the fixings in each of the ramekins. Sprinkle with the salt and pepper. Bake until set (20 min.).
4. Serve when they are to your liking.

Eggs in a Zucchini Nest

Yields: 4 Servings

Ingredients:

8 oz. grated zucchini
4 t. butter
¼ t. sea salt
½ t. of each:
-Black pepper
-Paprika
4 eggs
4 oz. shredded cheddar cheese

Also Needed: 4 ramekins

How to Prepare:

1. Warm up the Air Fryer at 356°F.
2. Grate the zucchini. Add the butter to the ramekins and add the zucchini in a nest shape. Sprinkle with the paprika, salt, and pepper.
3. Whisk the eggs and add to the nest, topping it off with the cheese.
4. Air fry 7 minutes. Chill for 3 minutes and serve in the ramekin.

French Toast Sticks

Yields: 2 Servings

Ingredients:

2 eggs
4 slices of desired bread
2 tbsp. soft margarine or butter
A pinch of each:
-Cinnamon
-Salt
-Ground cloves
-Nutmeg
Garnish: Maple syrup

How to Prepare:

1. Warm up the Air Fryer to 356°F.
2. Whisk the eggs. Give them a shake of nutmeg, cloves, and cinnamon.
3. Spread butter on both sides of the bread and cut them into strips. Dredge each of the pieces in the egg mixture and arrange in the fryer. (You will need to make two batches.)
4. Pause the fryer after two minutes, remove the pan, and spray the bread with cooking spray.
5. Flip and spray the other side, returning them to the AF for an additional four minutes, making sure they do not burn.
6. It's ready when it is golden brown.
7. Garnish with some maple syrup or whipped cream. Use a drizzle of some confectioner's sugar for a sweeter experience. Serve them immediately.

Mini Bacon Wrapped Burritos (Vegan)

Yields: 4 Servings

Ingredients:

2 servings Tofu Scramble or Vegan Egg
2-3 tbsp. tamari
2 tbsp. cashew butter
1-2 tbsp. each:
-Water
 -Liquid smoke
4 pieces of rice paper

Vegetable Add-Ins:

8 strips roasted red pepper
1/3 c. sweet potato roasted cubes
1 small sautéed tree broccoli
A small handful of greens
6-8 stalks of fresh asparagus

Note: You can substitute with spinach, kale, etc.

How to Prepare:

1. Line the pan used for baking with parchment. Preheat the Air Fryer to 350°F.
2. Whisk the tamari, cashew butter, water, and liquid smoke, and place it to the side.
3. *Prepare the Filling*: Hold a rice paper under cold running water—getting both sides wet—just a second. Place on the plate to fill.

4. Start by filling the ingredients –just off from the center—leaving the sides of the paper free.
5. Fold in two of the sides as you would when you make a burrito. Seal them and dip each one in the liquid smoke mixture—coating completely.
6. Cook until crispy, usually about eight to ten minutes.

Sausage Wraps

Yields: 8 Wraps

Ingredients:

1 can crescent roll dough (8 count)
2 slices American cheese
8 Heat & Serve Sausages
8 wooden skewers
For Dipping: Ketchup, syrup, or BBQ sauce

How to Prepare:

1. Cut the cheese into quarters. Open the sausages and separate the rolls.
2. Add the cheese strips starting on the widest part of the triangle to the tip. Add the sausage.
3. Pull up each of the ends of the roll over the sausage and cheese. Be sure to pinch all of the sides together and add these in two batches to the Air Fryer.
4. Set the AF to 380°F. Cook for three minutes, maybe four depending on how crispy you like the bread.
5. Remove from the fryer and add a skewer. Set it out for serving with the desired garnish.

Scrambled Eggs

Yields: 1 Serving

Ingredients:

2 eggs
Pepper and salt to taste

How to Prepare:

1. Program the Air Fryer to 284°F for about five minutes.
2. Put the butter in the fryer to melt and spread it out evenly.
3. Empty the eggs and any other ingredients such as cheese or tomatoes.
4. Open the fryer every few minutes to whisk the eggs to the desired yellow and fluffy consistency.
5. Have some toast on the side or have a scrambled egg sandwich.

Spinach Frittata

Yields: 1-2 Servings

Ingredients:

1/3 package of spinach - approximately
1 small minced red onion
Mozzarella cheese
3 eggs

How to Prepare:

1. Set the temperature of the Air Fryer at 356°F for at least three minutes.
2. Add oil to a baking pan for one minute.
3. Toss in the onions and continue cooking for two to three minutes. Toss in the spinach and cook three to five minutes additional minutes.
4. Whisk in the eggs and add the seasonings and cheese to the pan. Cook for eight minutes. Flavor the tasty treat with a bit of pepper and salt.

Chapter 3: Tasty Poultry Choices

From wings to breasts, you have the variety for some quick and easy meals in this segment!

Buffalo Chicken Wings

Yields: 2-3 Servings

Ingredients:

5 chicken wings (approx. 14 oz.)
Optional: ½ t. garlic powder
2 t. cayenne pepper
2 tbsp. red-hot sauce
1 tbsp. melted butter
Fresh black pepper and salt to taste

How to Prepare:

1. Preheat the Air Fryer at 356°F.
2. Cut the wings into three sections (the end tip, middle joint, and drumstick). Pat each one thoroughly dry using a paper towel. Wash your hands right away to prevent cross-contamination.
3. Combine a dash of pepper and salt, the garlic powder, and cayenne pepper in a plate. Lightly coat the wings with the powder.
4. Place the chicken on the wire rack and back for 15 minutes, turning once at 7 minutes.
5. Combine the hot sauce, and melted butter in a dish to garnish the baked chicken when it is time to be served.

Suggestion: You can increase the cayenne pepper if you want it hotter.

Chicken Curry

Yields: 4 Servings

Ingredients:

1 lb. chicken breast – no skin or bones
1 t. olive oil
1 onion
2 t. minced garlic
1 tbsp. of each:
 -Lemongrass
 -Apple cider vinegar
½ c. each:
 -Chicken stock
 -Coconut milk
2 tbsp. curry paste

How to Prepare:

1. Preheat the fryer to 365°F.
2. Chop the chicken into cubes. Peel and dice the onion and combine in the Air Fryer basket. Cook 5 minutes.
3. Remove and add the rest of the fixings. Mix well and cook another 10 minutes.
4. Serve and enjoy for lunch for a quick and healthy meal.

Chicken Fried Rice

Yields: 5-6 Servings

Ingredients:

1 c. frozen carrots and peas
3 c. cold cooked white rice
1 tbsp. vegetable oil
6 tbsp. soy sauce
1 c. – packed cooked chicken
½ c. diced onion
Also Needed: 7x2 cake pan

How to Prepare:
1. Cook and dice the chicken. Prepare the rice. Dice the onion.
2. Add the chilled white rice into a mixing container along with the soy sauce and oil. Mix well.
3. Toss in the onion, chicken, peas, and carrots. Stir well.
4. Combine the ingredients in the Air Fryer and cook 20 minutes at 360°F.
5. Serve as a side with your favorite meat or enjoy it alone.

Chicken Hash

Yields: 3 Servings

Ingredients:

7 oz. chicken fillet
6 oz. chopped cauliflower
½ yellow diced onion
1 chopped green pepper
1 tbsp. of each:
 -Water
 -Cream
1 t. black pepper
3 tbsp. butter

How to Prepare:

1. Program the Air Fryer to 380°F. Chop the cauliflower and add to a blender to make rice. Chop the chicken into bite-sized pieces and sprinkle with salt and pepper.
2. Prepare the veggies and combine the fixings.
3. Add the fryer basket and cook until done (6-7 min.). Check it often to prevent scorching.
4. Serve and enjoy.

Chicken Kabobs

Yields: 2 Servings

Ingredients:

3 bell peppers – multi colors of your choice
6 mushrooms
1/3 c. each of:
-Soy sauce
-Honey
Pepper and salt – to taste
Cooking oil spray
Sesame seeds
2 diced chicken breasts

How to Prepare

1. Chop the mushrooms into halves. Dice the chicken and peppers. Give the chicken a couple squirts of oil and a pinch of salt and pepper.
2. Combine the soy and honey – mixing well. Add some sesame seeds and stir.
3. Insert the peppers, chicken, and mushroom bits onto a skewer.
4. Set the temperature of the Air Fryer to 338°F. Cover the kabobs with the sauce and add them to the AF basket.
5. Cook for 15-20 minutes and serve.

Chicken Pot Pie

Yields: 4 Servings

Ingredients:

6 chicken tenders
 2 potatoes
1 ½ c. condensed cream of celery soup
¾ c. heavy cream
1 thyme sprig
1 whole dried bay leaf
5 refrigerated buttermilk biscuits
1 tbsp. milk
1 egg yolk

How to Prepare:

1. Preheat the Air Fryer at 320°F.
2. Remove the skin from the potatoes and dice.
3. Combine all of the ingredients in a pan except for the milk, egg yolk, and biscuits. Bring them to a boil using medium heat.
4. Empty the mixture into the baking tin and use some aluminum foil to cover the top. Place the pan into the fry basket using a sling. Set the timer for 15 minutes.
5. Meanwhile, after the pie completes the cycle make an egg wash with the milk and egg yolk. Place the biscuits on the baking pan and brush with the egg wash mixture.
6. Set the timer to 300°F for an additional ten minutes.
7. Your pie is ready when the biscuits are golden brown.

Chicken Strips

Yields: 4 Servings

Ingredients:

1 lb. chicken fillets
1 t. paprika
1 tbsp. cream
½ t. Salt & pepper

How to Prepare:

1. Dice the fillets into strips. Season to your liking with the salt and pepper.
2. Set the Air Fryer at 365°F and add the butter to the basket.
3. Arrange the strips in the basket and air fry for 6 minutes.
4. Flip the strips and cook for another 5 minutes.
5. When done, sprinkle with the cream and paprika. Serve warm.

Chicken Tenderloin

Yields: 4 Servings

Ingredients:

3 1/3 tbsp. breadcrumbs
2 tbsp. butter/vegetable oil
8 chicken tenderloins
1 egg

How to Prepare:

1. Set the temperature to 356ºF.
2. Combine the breadcrumbs and oil, stirring until the mix crumbles.
3. Whisk the egg. Run the chicken through the egg, shaking off the excess.
4. Dip the egged chicken into the crumbs to coat each piece evenly.
5. Organize them in the fryer for 12 minutes. The chicken is ready to eat from start to finish in 22 minutes. The time varies with the chicken thickness.

Chinese Chicken Wings

Yields: 2 Servings

Ingredients:

4 chicken wings
Salt and pepper to taste
1 tbsp. each:
 -Chinese spice
 -Mixed spice
 -Soy sauce

How to Prepare:

1. Warm up the AF to 356°F.
2. Add the seasonings into a large mixing container—stirring thoroughly.

3. Blend the seasonings over the chicken wings until each piece is covered.
4. Put some aluminum foil on the base of the AF (similar to how you cover a baking tray), and add the chicken sprinkling any remnants over the chicken. Cook for 15 minutes.
5. Flip the chicken and cook another 15 minutes at 392°F.

Country-Style Chicken Tenders

Yields: 3-4 Servings

Ingredients:

¾ lb. chicken tenders
2 tbsp. olive oil
½ t. salt
2 beaten eggs
½ c. of each:
 -All-purpose flour
 -Seasoned breadcrumbs
1 t. black pepper

How to Prepare:

1. Preheat the Air Fryer heat to 330°F.
2. Set up three separate dishes for the flour, eggs, and breadcrumbs.
3. Blend the salt, pepper, and breadcrumbs. Pour in the oil with the breadcrumbs and mix. Put the chicken tenders into the flour, and the eggs. Coat evenly with the breadcrumbs. Shake the excess off before placing in the Air Fryer basket.
4. Cook for ten minutes at 330°F and increase to 390°F for five minutes or until they are a nice golden brown.

Fried Chicken

Ingredients:

2 chicken thighs - no skin
3 sprigs fresh parsley
Garlic powder – for dusting
Salt and black pepper if desired
½ a lemon
Chili flakes to our liking
1 to 2 sprigs fresh rosemary

How to Prepare:

1. Rinse the thighs. Drain them between two paper towels.
2. Clean the rosemary sprigs and remove the stems. Chop or mince the parsley.
3. *For the Marinade*: Combine the salt and pepper, garlic powder, rosemary leaves, parsley, chili flakes, and lemon juice. Add the thighs and marinate overnight in the refrigerator.
4. Preheat the Air Fryer: Set the AF to 356°F. Grill for 12 minutes.

Cooking Note: Times may vary depending on the thickness/size of the thighs.

Jamaican Chicken Meatballs

Yields: 10 Servings

Ingredients:

1 large peeled and diced onion
2 large chicken breasts
1 t. chili powder
2 tbsp. honey
Pepper and salt to taste
3 tbsp. soy sauce
1 tbsp. each:
 -Dry mustard
 -Cumin
 -Thyme
 -Basil
Optional: 2 t. Jerk Paste

How to Prepare:

1. Using a blender, mince the chicken, add the onion, and mince. Mix well. Toss in the Jamaican seasonings and blend again. Make ten medium balls.
2. Place the balls on the baking mat in the AF and cook at 356°F.
3. Place them on a stick when done with the cooking and pour some of the extra sauce over the meatballs.
4. Add several herbs on the top, serve, and enjoy.

Note: Jerk paste is a combination of brown spices, peppers, ginger, and thyme.

Lemon & Rosemary Chicken

Yields: 4-6 Servings

Ingredients:

1 lb. chicken

For the Marinade:

1 tbsp. soy sauce
½ tbsp. olive oil
1 t. minced ginger

For the Sauce:

3 tbsp. brown sugar
1 tbsp. oyster sauce
½ of lemon in skins (wedge-cut)
Optional: 15 g (0.5 oz.) fresh rosemary

How to Prepare:

1. Leave the skin on the rosemary and chop.
2. Blend all of the marinade components. Pour over the chicken. Let them cool off in the fridge for about thirty minutes.
3. Place the marinade and chicken in a baking container and bake for six minutes in the AF at 392°F.
4. Blend all of the sauce ingredients (minus the lemon). Pour the mixture over the chicken when it is about half-baked.
5. Place the lemon wedges in the pan evenly and squeeze so the zest will heighten the flavor of the chicken. Continue baking for an additional 13 minutes turning to ensure all of the pieces are browned evenly.

Old Bay Chicken Wings

Yields: 4 Servings

Ingredients

3 lb. chicken wing parts
1 tbsp. Old Bay Seasoning
3/4 c. potato starch
½ c. butter
Fresh lemons
1 t. True Lemon or more juice of a lemon to taste

How to Prepare:

1. Warm up the Air Fryer to 360°F.
2. Rinse and dry the wings with some paper towels.
3. Combine with the seasoning and potato starch. Add the wings. Coat and cook for 35 minutes. Shake the basket often.
4. Melt the butter and add it along with the True Lemon. Add it to the hot wings.
5. Stir and add the rest of the lemon butter and lemons for squeezing.

Orange Chicken Wings

Yields: 2 Servings

Ingredients:

1 orange – zest and juiced
6 chicken wings
1 ½ tbsp. Worcestershire sauce
1 tbsp. sugar
Herbs: Sage, thyme, basil, mint, parsley, oregano, etc.
Pepper to taste

How to Prepare:

1. Prepare the wings and pour the juice and zest into a bowl. Add the remainder of the ingredients and rub in. Let it marinate for 30 minutes.
2. Program the temperature on the Air Fryer to 356°F.
3. Combine the wings and juices together. Add to the fryer basket for 20 minutes.
4. Remove the wings from the fryer, discard the zest, and brush ½ of the sauce over the wings. Return to the fryer and cook an additional ten minutes.
5. Add the wings to a serving platter and enjoy!

Tarragon Chicken

Yields: 1 Serving

Ingredients:

1 skinless and boneless chicken breast
⅛ t. of each:
-Kosher salt
- Freshly cracked ground black pepper
½ t. unsalted butter
¼ c. dried tarragon
12"x14" piece aluminum foil

How to Prepare:

1. Set the temperature in advance to 390°F.
2. Place the chicken in the foil and add the tarragon and butter with a sprinkle of salt and pepper.
3. Loosely wrap the foil for minimal airflow. Air fry for 12 minutes in the basket.
4. Serve it up and enjoy.

Whole Chicken: Rotisserie Style

Yields: 4 Servings

Ingredients:

Olive oil- as needed
1 (6-7 lb.) whole chicken
Seasoned salt

Note: Under 6 lb. - use a 3.7-quart Air Fryer.

How to Prepare:

1. Clean and dry the chicken and coat with the oil. Season with the salt.
2. Arrange the chicken in the Air Fryer – skin-side down.
3. Cook at 350°F for 30 minutes. Turn it over and continue cooking another 30 minutes.
4. Serve any way you like it.

Turkey Specialties

Avocado & Turkey Burrito

Yields: 2 Servings

Ingredients:

4 eggs
Pepper & Salt – to taste
4 tbsp. salsa
8 slices cooked turkey breast
½ c. sliced avocado
¼ c. mozzarella cheese -grated
½ sliced red bell pepper
2 tortillas

How to Prepare:

1. Whisk the eggs with the pepper and salt. Spray the Air Fryer tray with some non-stick cooking oil. Add the eggs.
2. Prepare at 390°F for 5 minutes. Scrape the bowl and add the eggs to the tortillas.
3. Layer the turkey, avocado, peppers, cheese, and salsa. Roll it up slowly.
4. Spray the fryer and arrange the burritos in the basket. Prepare for 5 minutes.
5. Serve warm and enjoy when you're in a hurry.

Mozzarella Turkey Rolls

Yields: 4 Servings

Ingredients:

1 sliced tomato
4 slices turkey breast
½ c. freshly chopped basil
1 c. sliced mozzarella
4 chive shoots – for tying

How to Prepare:

1. Warm up the Air Fryer to 390F.
2. On each slice of turkey, add a slice of cheese, tomato, and basil.
3. Roll up each one and tie them with the chive shoot.
4. Add to the fryer for 10 minutes. Prepare and serve warm.

Roast Turkey Breast

Yields: 8-10 Servings

Ingredients:

1 tbsp. ground black pepper
8 lb. bone-in turkey breast
2 tbsp. each:
-Olive oil
-Sea salt

How to Prepare:

1. Program the Air Fryer on 360°F.
2. Rub the turkey with olive oil and flavor with the seasonings.
3. Put the turkey in the preheated basket for 20 minutes.
4. When done, flip it over and adjust the cooking time for another 20 minutes (also at 360°F).
5. The breast of turkey is done when it indicates 165°F when tested with a meat thermometer.
6. Allow the meat to rest a minimum of 20 minutes before serving.

Roast Turkey Reuben

Yields: 2 Servings

Ingredients:

4 slices rye bread
8 slices skinless – roasted turkey breast
4 tbsp. coleslaw
8 slices Swiss cheese
2 tbsp. each of:
 -Salted butter
 -Russian dressing

How to Prepare:

1. Prepare two slices of the bread on one side with butter and lay them – butter side down- on the cutting board.
2. In layers, arrange the turkey, cheese, coleslaw, and Russian dressing on top of the two slices of bread. Fold them together to make one sandwich.
3. Add the sandwich to the Air Fryer basket.
4. Push 'm' and choose the bake icon setting it to 310°F for 12 minutes.
5. After six minutes, flip the sandwich, and continue until browned.
6. When done, slice and serve.

Turkey Breast with Maple Mustard Glaze

Yields: 6 Servings

Ingredients:

2 t. olive oil
1 (5 lb.) whole turkey breast
1 t. of each:
-Salt
-Dried thyme
-Butter
½ t. of each:
-Freshly cracked black pepper
-Smoked paprika
-Dried sage
¼ c. maple syrup
2 tbsp. Dijon mustard

How to Prepare:

1. Before you begin, preheat the fryer to 350°F.
2. Prepare the breast with a coating of olive oil.
3. Mix the sage, thyme, pepper, salt, and paprika as a rub. Use it as a spice coating for the turkey.
4. Add the breast in the fryer basket and air fry for 25 minutes. Rotate it on its side and fry another 12 minutes. It's done when it reaches 165°F – internal temperature.
5. Meanwhile, whisk the butter, syrup, and mustard in a saucepan. Turn the breast again and brush the glaze over the breast. Give it a final five minutes until crispy brown.
6. Cover it with a foil tent for five minutes, slice, and serve.

Chapter 4: Beef Specialties

Wait 'til you try these tasty dishes!

Beef Roll-Ups

Yields: 4 Servings

Ingredients:

6 slices provolone cheese
2 lbs. beef flank steak
3 tbsp. pesto
¾ c. fresh baby spinach
3 oz. roasted red bell peppers
1 t. of each:
-Black pepper
-Sea salt

How to Prepare:

1. Open the steak (4 pieces) and spread the pesto, layer the cheese, spinach, and peppers ¾ down the meat.
2. Roll it up and secure it with toothpicks. Sprinkle it with some pepper and salt.
3. Set the Air Fryer to 400°F. Cook the roll-ups 14 minutes, rotating halfway through the process.
4. Let them rest ten minutes. Slice and serve.

Beef Stew

Yields: 6 Servings

Ingredients:

2 t. butter
10 oz. beef short ribs
½ t. chili flakes
1 t. turmeric
¼ t. salt
1 c. chicken stock
½ onion
1 green pepper
4 oz. of each:
- Kale
-Green peas

How to Prepare:

1. Program the Air Fryer to 360°F.
2. Add the butter to melt in the fryer basket and place the ribs.
3. Sprinkle with the chili flakes, salt, and turmeric. Cook for 15 minutes.
4. Remove the seeds and chop the green pepper and kale. Dice the onion.
5. When the timer buzzes, pour in the stock along with the peppers and onions. Sprinkle with the peas and add the peeled garlic clove.
6. Stir well and add the chopped kale. Cook 8 more minutes.
7. Let the stew steep for a short while to blend all the delicious flavors.
8. Serve and relax.

Country Fried Steak

Yields: 1 Serving

Ingredients:

1 (6 oz.) sirloin steak
3 beaten eggs
1 c. of each:
-Panko
-Flour
1 t. of each:
-Pepper
-Salt
-Garlic powder
-Onion powder
6 oz. ground sausage
1 t. pepper
2 tbsp. flour
2 c. milk

How to Prepare:

1. Use a meat mallet to beat the steak until thin. Add the seasonings with the panko.
2. Dredge the beef through the flour, egg, and panko.
3. Place the steak in the basket. Set the temperature to 370°F. It should take 12 minutes. Remove the steak.
4. *For the Gravy:* Cook the sausage and drain, saving two tablespoons in the pan. Blend in the flour along with the sausage and mix well.
5. Pour in the milk and mix until thickened. Add a sprinkle of pepper and cook approximately three more minutes.
6. Enjoy with a serving of gravy.

Rib Steak

Yields: 2 Servings

Ingredients:

1 tbsp. of steak rub
2 lb. rib steaks
1 tbsp. of olive oil

How to Prepare:

1. Before it is time to cook, preheat the Air Fryer to 400°F.
2. Flavor the meat on all areas with the oil and rub.
3. Put it in the basket for 14 minutes, flipping after seven minutes.
4. Let it rest for at least ten minutes before you slice and serve.

Roast Beef for Lunchtime Sandwiches

Yields: 6 Servings

Ingredients:

½ t. of each:
-Oregano
-Garlic powder
1 t. dried thyme
1 tbsp. olive oil
2 lb. round roast

How to Prepare:

1. Heat up the Air Fryer to 330°F.
2. Combine the spices. Brush the oil over the beef and rub in the spice mixture.
3. Add to a baking dish and place in the fryer for 30 minutes. Turn it over and continue cooking 25 more minutes.
4. Let it rest for a few minutes before slicing.
5. Serve on your choice of keto-friendly bread or eat it as it is.

Spicy Shredded Beef

Yields: 8 Servings

Ingredients:

1 t. of each:
-Thyme
-Salt
-Ground black pepper
-Mustard
-Dried dill
2 lb. beef steak
4 c. chicken stock
3 tbsp. butter
1 peeled garlic clove
1 bay leaf

How to Prepare:

1. Heat the Air Fryer in advance (350°F).
2. Whisk the egg and add the stevia, baking powder, and butter.
3. Reserve 1 t. of the almond flour and add the rest to the mixture. Knead until it's smooth and not sticky.
4. Line the fryer basket with parchment paper and add the prepared crust. Flatten and place the berries on top. Sprinkle with (1 t.) the almond flour.
5. Prepare the pie in the Air Fryer for 20 minutes and remove when it's golden brown.
6. Chill and slice for your awaiting guests. Add a tasty salad and enjoy.

The Steak Rub

Ingredients:

1 tbsp. packed brown sugar
2 tbsp. granulated sugar
1 ½ tbsp. each:
 -Ground cumin
 -Chili powder
 -Paprika
 -Garlic powder
1 t. each:
 -Onion powder
 -Salt
 -Ground black pepper
 -White pepper

How to Prepare:

1. Combine the fixings and rub your favorite meats.

Steak – Medium-Rare

Yields: 1 Serving

Ingredients:

1 (1 ½-inch) beef steak
Pepper and salt – to taste
Olive oil

How to Prepare:

1. Warm up the fryer to 350ºF.
2. Oil the steak and season with the pepper and salt.
3. Arrange the prepared beef in the tray and cook 3 minutes per side.

Ground Beef Choices

Beef & Bacon Taco Rolls

Yields: 2 Servings

Ingredients:

2 c. ground beef
To Taste - with the beef taco spices:
 -Garlic powder
 -Chili powder
 -Black pepper
½ c. bacon bits
1 c. of each:
 -Tomato salsa
 -Shredded Monterey Jack Cheese
4 turmeric coconut wraps/your choice

How to Prepare:

1. Heat the fryer to 390°F.
2. Season the beef with the spices. Add all of the fixings into the wraps.
3. Roll up the wraps and arrange them in the Air Fryer.
4. Air fry for 15 minutes and serve.

Beef & Potatoes

Yields: 4 Servings

Ingredients:

1 lb. ground beef
3 c. mashed potatoes
2 eggs
2 tbsp. garlic powder
1 c. sour cream
To Taste: Freshly cracked black pepper
Pinch of salt

How to Prepare:

1. Preheat the Air Fryer to 390°F.
2. Combine all of the fixings in a mixing bowl and place in heat-safe dish.
3. Place in the fryer for 2- minutes.
4. Enjoy when you want a bit more than a sandwich for lunch.

Beef Empanadas

Yields: 4 Servings

Ingredients:

2 cloves of garlic
1 small onion
1 lb. ground beef
1 pkg. empanada shells
1 tbsp. olive oil
½ green pepper
½ t. cumin
¼ c. tomato salsa
1 egg yolk
To Taste: Pepper & Sea salt

How to Prepare:

1. Peel and mince the onion and garlic. Deseed and dice the pepper.
2. Add the oil to a sauté pan over high heat. Cook the ground beef until brown, drain the grease, and add the onions and garlic. Cook for 4 minutes. Combine the remainder of ingredients (omit the milk, egg, and shells). Cook on low for 10 minutes.
3. Make an egg wash with the yolk and milk.
4. Add the meat to ½ of the rolled dough brushing the edges with the wash. Fold it over and seal with the fork, brushing with the wash, and adding it to the basket.
5. Continue the process until all are done. Cook in the AF for 10 minutes at 350°F.

Beef Schnitzel

Yields: 1 Serving

Ingredients:

2 tbsp. olive oil
1 thin beef schnitzel
½ c. gluten-free breadcrumbs
1 egg

How to Prepare:

1. Warm up the Air Fryer a couple of minutes (356ºF).
2. Combine the oil and breadcrumbs in a shallow bowl. Whisk the egg in another mixing bowl.
3. Dip the beef into the egg, and then the breadcrumbs. Arrange in the preheated basket of the Air Fryer.
4. Fry 12 minutes and serve.

Cheeseburgers Inside Out

Yields: 4 Servings

Ingredients:

¾ lb. or 12 oz. lean ground beef
4 t. ketchup
3 tbsp. minced onion
2 t. yellow mustard
Fresh ground black pepper
 Salt
8 dill pickle chips
4 slices cheddar cheese

How to Prepare:

1. Set the Air Fryer to 370°F.
2. Break the cheese into small bits.
3. In a large container, mix the ketchup, ground beef, pepper, salt, and mustard. Make four patties. Place two side by side.
4. Flatten the patty and add four pickle chips. Add a layer of cheese, add a patty, and press the meat together tightly to keep the contents intact while cooking.
5. Arrange the burgers in the basket and air-fry for twenty minutes. Flip after about ten minutes.
6. Enjoy with a bun, tomato, and some lettuce.

Cheeseburger Mini Sliders

Yields: 3 Large Servings

Ingredients:

6 slices cheddar cheese
1 lb. ground beef
6 dinner rolls
Black pepper and Salt

How to Prepare:

1. Program the heat setting on the Air Fryer to 390°F.
2. Form 6 (2 ½-oz.) patties and flavor with the pepper and salt.
3. Place the burgers on the AF basket for ten minutes.
4. Take them from the cooker and add the cheese. Return them to the Air Fryer for an additional minute until the cheese melts.
1.

Cheeseburger Patties

Yields: 6 Servings

Ingredients:

1 lb. ground beef
Salt
Black pepper
6 slices cheddar cheese

How to Prepare:

1. Program the Air Fryer. Combine the fixings and mix well.
2. Shape into six burgers.
3. Air fry for 10 minutes and enjoy!

Maggi Hamburgers

Yields: 4 Servings

Ingredients:

1 t. of each:
-Maggi seasoning sauce - located at Walmart
 -Dried parsley
1 tbsp. Worcestershire sauce
1-2 drops liquid smoke
½ t. of each:
 -Dried oregano
 -Ground black pepper
 -Salt substitute
 -Onion powder
 -Garlic powder
1 lb. – 93% lean ground beef

How to Prepare:

1. Set the temperature in the Air Fryer to 350ºF.
2. Combine all of the seasonings in a small dish and blend in the beef. Mix well until just combined.
3. Make four patties and arrange them on the tray together. Cook for ten minutes – depending on the desired doneness. You don't need to flip them. Enjoy!

Meatloaf with Black Peppercorns

Yields: 4 Servings

Ingredients:

4 ½ lb. ground beef
Breadcrumbs – if homemade/one slice of bread
1 t. Worcestershire sauce
3 tbsp. tomato ketchup
1 large onion – diced
1 tbsp. of each:
-Basil
-Oregano
-Parsley
Salt and pepper

How to Prepare:

1. Set the temperature to at 356°F.
2. Toss the beef into a large mixing container and blend in the herbs, onion, Worcestershire sauce, and ketchup. Mix well for about five minutes, add the breadcrumbs, and combine well.
3. Add the meatloaf to the baking dish and place in the fryer. Cook for 25 minutes.

Taco Fried Egg Rolls

Yields: 8 Servings

Ingredients:

1 lb. lean (93%) ground beef
½ of an onion – chopped
16 egg roll wrappers
1 can - Cilantro Lime Rotel
½ pkg. taco seasoning
½ can fat-free refried black beans
1 tbsp. olive oil
1 c. reduced-fat Mexican cheese
½ c. frozen whole kernel corn

How to Prepare:

1. Set the fryer temperature to 400°F.
2. Prepare a frying pan using the med-high heat setting to sauté the garlic and onions.
3. Toss in the beef, seasoning pack, salt, and pepper.
4. Blend in the corn, beans, and Rotel.
5. Prepare the wrappers on a flat surface. Glaze the wrappers with a brush dipped in water along the edges to make the roll easier to close.
6. Load them up and use two wrappers for this amount of beef. Sprinkle each one with some cheese. Roll them up and tuck in each end. Spray with some olive oil.
7. Add to the fryer and cook for eight minutes. Flip the rolls over and cook for another four minutes. The time may vary – depending on the size of the cooker.
8. Note: You don't need to double wrap, but it will be a bit messy.

Chapter 5: Pork & Fish Choices

Delicious Pork Favorites

Bacon-Wrapped Pork Tenderloin

Yields: 4-6 Servings

Ingredients:

3-4 bacon strips
1 pork tenderloin
1-2 tbsp. Dijon mustard

How to Prepare:

1. Coat the tenderloin with the mustard and wrap with the bacon.
2. Set the Air Fryer at 360ºF for 15 minutes. Flip and cook 10-15 more minutes.
3. Serve with your favorite sides.

Crispy Breaded Pork Chops

Yields: 6 Servings

Ingredients:

6 (3/4-inch) center-cut boneless chops
1 large egg
3/4 t. kosher salt
1/2 c. panko crumbs
1/3 c. crushed cornflakes
1 1/4 t. sweet paprika
2 tbsp. grated parmesan cheese
1/2 t. of each powder:
 -Onion
 -Garlic
1/4 t. chili powder
1/8 t. freshly cracked black pepper

How to Prepare:

1. Warm up the Air Fryer (12 min.) to 400°F. Lightly spray the basket with cooking spray.
2. Shake the salt over the chops.
3. Mix the cornflake crumbs, panko, the kosher salt, pepper, and chili powder.
4. Whisk the egg in another container and dip the pork. Next, dip in the crumb mixture and add to the basket.
5. Prepare in 2 batches. Cook 12 minutes – flipping halfway through the cycle. Spritz both sides of the chops before browning.

Raspberry Balsamic Smoked Pork Chops

Yields: 4 Servings

Ingredients:

2 large eggs
1 c. of each:
 -Japanese – panko breadcrumbs
 -Finely chopped pecans
1/4 c. of each:
 -2% milk
 -All-purpose flour
4 smoked bone-in pork chops
1/3 c. balsamic vinegar
2 tbsp. of each:
 -Seedless raspberry jam
 -Brown sugar
1 tbsp. thawed frozen orange juice concentrate

How to Prepare:

1. Warm up the Air Fryer to 400°F. Spritz the basket with cooking spray.
2. Whisk the milk and eggs in one dish and combine the pecans and breadcrumbs in another.
3. Prepare in batches. Dip in the flour, shaking off the excess. Dip them into the egg mix.
4. Prepare in single layers in the fryer 12-15 minutes, turning about 1/2 way through the cooking cycle.
5. Combine the rest of the fixings in a small saucepan, bringing it to a boil. Simmer 6-8 minutes until thickened. Serve over the chops.

Roast Pork Loin with Red Potatoes

Yields: 2 Servings

Ingredients:

2 large red potatoes
2 lb. pork loin
1 t. of each:
-Pepper
-Salt
-Parsley
½ t. of each:
-Red pepper flakes
-Garlic powder
Balsamic glaze from cooking

How to Prepare:

1. Dice the potatoes.
2. Combine all of the seasonings and sprinkle over the potatoes and loin.
3. Arrange the pork and then the potatoes in the air fryer.
4. Secure the top and choose the roast button. Set the timer for 25 minutes.
5. When done, let it rest for several minutes before slicing.
6. Meanwhile, pour the roasted potatoes into the serving dishes.
7. Slice the loin into 4-5 sections. Use a balsamic glaze over the pork.

Southern Fried Pork Chops

Yields: 4 Servings

Ingredients:

4 pork chops
3 tbsp. buttermilk
1/4 c. all-purpose flour
To Your Liking:
 -Seasoning salt
 -Pepper
Cooking oil spray

How to Prepare:

1. Rinse and pat dry the chops. Season with the pepper and salt. Drizzle the chops with the buttermilk and place in a Ziploc-type bag with the flour. Toss well. Marinate 30 minutes.
2. Arrange the chops in the fryer. You can stack if needed. Spritz with the cooking oil.
3. Air fry for 15 minutes (380°F). Flip after the first 10 minutes.
4. Serve this southern delight with your favorite sides.
2.

Fish & Seafood

Breaded Fried Shrimp

Yields: 4 Servings

Ingredients:

3 tbsp. or 1 egg white
1 lb. raw shrimp
½ c. all-purpose flour
¾ c. panko breadcrumbs
1 t. paprika
Pepper and salt to your liking
McCormick's Grill Makes Montreal Chicken Seasoning
Cooking spray

Ingredients for the Sauce:

2 tbsp. Sriracha
1/3 c. plain non-fat Greek yogurt
¼ c. sweet chili sauce

How to Prepare:

1. Peel and devein the shrimp.
2. Warm up the Air Fryer to 400°F.
3. Add the seasonings to the shrimp.
4. Use three bowls for the breadcrumbs, egg whites, and flour.
5. Dip the shrimp into the flour, the egg, and lastly the breadcrumbs.
6. Lightly spray the shrimp and add to the fryer basket for four minutes. Flip the shrimp over and cook for another

four minutes. Watch the last few minutes to prevent burning.

7. For the Sauce: Combine all of the fixings and combine thoroughly.

Cajun Salmon

Yields: 1-2 Servings

Ingredients:

1 salmon fillet – ¾-inches thick
Juice of ¼ lemon
Cajun seasoning for coating
Optional: Sprinkle of sugar

How to Prepare:

1. Preheat the AF to 356°F. The process usually takes about five minutes.
2. Rinse and pat the salmon dry. Thoroughly coat the fish with the coating mix.
3. Arrange the fillet in the fryer for seven minutes with the skin side up.
4. Serve with a sprinkle of the lemon.

Cajun Shrimp

Yields: 4-6 Servings

Ingredients:

1 tbsp. olive oil
½ t. Old Bay seasoning
16-20 (1 ¼ lb.) tiger shrimp
¼ t. each:
 -Smoked paprika
 -Cayenne pepper
1 pinch of salt

How to Prepare:

1. Preheat the Air Fryer to 390°F.
2. Mix all of the ingredients and coat the shrimp with the oil and spices.
3. Place the shrimp in the basket and cook for five minutes.
4. Complement the meal with some rice and put the shrimp on top for a tasty luncheon treat.

Catfish

Yields: 3 Servings

Ingredients:

1 tbsp. olive oil
¼ c. seasoned fish fry
4 catfish fillets

How to Prepare:

1. Prepare the fryer to 400°F.
2. Rinse the fish and pat them dry with a towel.
3. Empty the seasoning into a large zipper type baggie. Add the fish and shake to cover each fillet. Spray them with some oil and add to the basket.
4. Cook for ten minutes, flip, and cook for ten more minutes. Flip once more and cook for two to three minutes.
5. Once it reaches the desired crispiness, remove, and enjoy.

Clams Oregano

Yields: 4 Servings

Ingredients:

2 dozen shucked clams
1 c. unseasoned breadcrumbs
4 tbsp. melted butter
3 minced garlic cloves
1 t. dried oregano
¼ c. of each:
 -Chopped parsley
 -Grated parmesan cheese

For the Pan: 1 c. sea salt

How to Prepare:

1. Warm up the Air Fryer a few minutes at 400°F.
2. Mix the breadcrumbs, oregano, parsley, parmesan cheese, and melted butter in a medium mixing bowl.
3. Using a heaping tablespoon of the crumb mixture, add it to the clams.
4. Fill the insert with the salt, arrange the clams inside, and air fry for three minutes.
5. Garnish with some lemon wedges and fresh parsley.

Coconut Shrimp

Yields: 3 Servings

Ingredients:

12 - large shrimp
1 c. of each:
-Gluten-free flour
-Gluten-free breadcrumbs
-Egg white
-Coconut – Unsweetened + Dried
1 tbsp. cornstarch

How to Prepare:

1. Program the Air Fryer to 350°F.
2. Preparation Steps: Prepare a shallow platter and combine the breadcrumbs and coconut. In another bowl, mix the cornstarch and flour. Add the egg to a small bowl.
3. Coat the shrimp with the egg white, flour, and lastly – the breadcrumbs.
4. Arrange in the fryer basket for 10 minutes.
5. Serve with your favorite sides or enjoy as a quick snack.

Cod Steaks with Ginger

Yields: 2 Servings

Ingredients:

2 slices large cod steaks
¼ t. turmeric powder
1 Pinch of salt & pepper
½ t. of each:
-Ginger powder
-Garlic powder
1 tbsp. plum sauce
Ginger slices
1 part of Kentucky Kernel Seasoned Flour (+) 1 part of corn flour

How to Prepare:

1. Dry off the cod steaks and marinate with the ginger powder, pepper, salt, and turmeric powder for a few minutes.
2. Lightly coat each of the steaks with the cornflour and Kentucky mix.
3. Set the temperature in the AF to 356°F for 15 minutes and increase to 400°F for 5 minutes. (Time may vary depending on the size of the cod.)
4. Prepare the sauce in a wok. Brown the ginger slices and remove from the heat. Add the plum sauce. You can dilute the sauce with a small amount of water if desired.
5. Serve the steaks with a drizzle of the tasty sauce.

Cod Sticks

Yields: 5 Servings

Ingredients:

3 tbsp. milk
2 large eggs
2 c. breadcrumbs
¼ t. salt
½ t. black pepper
1 c. almond flour
1 lb. cod

How to Prepare:

1. Program the Air Fryer to 350°F.
2. Prepare 3 bowls; 1 with the milk and eggs; 1 with the pepper, salt, and breadcrumbs; and another with almond flour.
3. Dip the sticks in the flour, egg mixture, and the breadcrumbs.
4. Place in the basket 12 minutes – shaking halfway through the air frying process.
5. Serve with your favorite sauce.

Crumbled Fish

Yields: 2 Servings

Ingredients:

½ c. breadcrumbs
4 tbsp. vegetable oil
1 whisked egg
4 fish fillets
To Serve: 1 lemon

How to Prepare:

1. Heat the Air Fryer to 356°F.
2. Mix the oil and breadcrumbs until it is crumbly. Dip the fish into the egg, then the crumb mix.
3. Arrange it in the fryer and cook for 12 minutes. Garnish with the lemon.

Dill Salmon

Yields: 4 Servings

Ingredients for the Salmon:

4 (6-oz. pieces) or 1 ½ lb. salmon
1 pinch of salt
2 t. olive oil

Ingredients for the Dill Sauce:

½ c. each:
-Sour cream
-Non-fat Greek yogurt
2 (finely chopped) tbsp. dill
1 Pinch of salt

How to Prepare:

1. Preheat the AF to 270°F.
2. Slice the salmon into the four portions, and drizzle with half of the oil (1 teaspoon). Flavor with a pinch of salt and add to the basket for about 20 to 23 minutes.
3. *Make the Sauce*: Blend the sour cream, yogurt, salt, and dill in a mixing container. Pour the sauce over the cooked salmon as a garnish with a pinch of the chopped dill.

Fish & Chips

Yields: 4 Servings

Ingredients:

2 catfish fillets (or similar fish)
3 slices wholemeal bread (for breadcrumbs)
1 med. beaten egg
1 (0.88 oz. approximately/25g) bag tortilla chips
Juice and rind of 1 lemon
Pepper and salt
1 tbsp. parsley

How to Prepare:

1. Set the fryer to 356°F.
2. Slice the fillets into four pieces ready for cooking. Flavor each one with the juice and set them aside.
3. Use a food processor for the tortillas, breadcrumbs, parsley, pepper, and lemon rind.
4. Cover each piece of the fish with the egg mix, then, run it through the crumb mixture.
5. Arrange them on the baking tray and cook until crispy.
6. Preparation time is ten minutes with a total cooking time of fifteen minutes.

Fish Tacos

Yields: 6 Servings

Ingredients:

1 c. tempura batter – made from:
-1 c. flour
-1 tbsp. cornstarch
½ c. of each:
-Cold seltzer water
-Salsa
1 c. coleslaw
1 t. white pepper
2 tbsp. chopped cilantro
½ c. guacamole
1 lemon – wedges

How to Prepare:

1. Make the tempura batter. Add a pinch of salt to the mixture to make it smooth.
2. Slice the cod into two-ounce pieces and give them a sprinkle of salt and pepper.
3. Use the batter (step 1) to coat the cod. Dredge them in the panko.
4. Use the French fry setting and cook for ten minutes. Turn after five minutes.
5. Garnish with some of the coleslaw, guacamole, cilantro, salsa, or some lemon.

Grilled Prawns/Shrimp

Yields: 4 Servings

Ingredients:

8 med. shrimp/prawns
1 tbsp. melted butter
1 rosemary sprig
Pepper & Salt – to your liking
3 minced garlic cloves

How to Prepare:

1. Combine all of the components in a mixing bowl. Toss well and arrange in the fryer basket.
2. Air fry the prawns for 7 minutes and serve.

Halibut Steak with a Teriyaki Glazed Sauce

Yields: 3 Servings

Ingredients:

1 lb. Halibut steak

Ingredients for the Marinade:

2/3 c. low-sodium soy sauce
½ c. Mirin Japanese cooking wine
¼ c. of each:
-Sugar
-Orange juice
2 tbsp. lime juice
¼ t. each:
-Ground ginger

-Crushed red pepper flakes
1 smashed garlic clove

How to Prepare:

1. Preheat the Air Fryer to 390°F.
2. Mix all of the marinade components in a pan, bringing it to a boil. Reduce the temperature to medium and then cool.
3. Pour half of the marinade in a plastic bag with the halibut and zip it closed. Chill in the fridge for thirty minutes.
4. Cook the halibut for ten to twelve minutes. Brush some of the remaining glaze mixture over the steak.
5. Serve over the top a bed of rice. Add a little basil or mint for some extra flavoring.

Lemon Fish

Yields: 4 Servings

Ingredients:

2 catfish cut into 4 pieces
Juice of 1 lemon
¼ c. sugar
2 t. green chili sauce
Salt to taste
1 egg white
4 t. corn flour slurry
1 t. red chili sauce
2-3 lettuce leaves
For Brushing: 2 tsp. oil

How to Prepare:

1. Boil ½ cup of water in a pan and add the sugar. Slice the lemon and place it in a dish.
2. Add the egg white, two teaspoons of oil, green sauce, salt, and flour in a bowl, mixing well. Add three tablespoons of water and whisk to make a smooth slurry batter.
3. Add some flour to a plate. Dip in the batter and then the flour.
4. Lightly grease the air fryer basket with a little oil and heat to 356°F.
5. Arrange the fillets in the basket and cook for 15-20 minutes until crispy.
6. Add salt to the pan (step 2) and stir well. Add the cornflour slurry and mix again. Blend in the red sauce juice, and lemon slices, mixing well and cooking until thickened.

7. Remove the fish from the basket, brush with some oil, and place back into the pan. Cook for about five more minutes.
8. Tear the leaves apart to make a serving bed. Add the fish and pour the lemon sauce over the top of the fish.
9. Serve and enjoy!

Salmon Croquettes

Yields: 4 Servings

Ingredients:

1 lb. (can) red salmon
1 c. breadcrumbs
1/3 c. vegetable oil
½ bunch chopped parsley
2 eggs

How to Prepare:

1. Set the Air Fryer at 392°F.
2. Drain and mash the salmon. Combine with the beaten eggs and parsley.
3. In another dish, mix the oil and breadcrumbs.
4. Make 16 croquettes with the mixture and coat with the breadcrumbs.
5. Arrange in the preheated basket 7 minutes.
6. Enjoy for lunch or any other time you want something new.

Salmon Patties

Yields: 6-8 Servings

Ingredients:

1 salmon portion (about 7 oz.)
3 large russet potatoes (about 14 oz.)
1/3 c. frozen veggies (parboiled and drained)
2 dill sprinkles
Dash of salt and pepper
1 egg

Ingredients for the Coating:

Breadcrumbs
Olive oil spray

How to Prepare:

1. Set the Air Fryer to 356°F.
2. Peel and chop the potatoes into small bits and boil for about ten minutes.
3. Mash and place in the fridge to chill.
4. Grill the salmon for five minutes, flake it apart, and set it to the side.
5. Combine all of the ingredients and shape into patties.
6. Evenly coat with the breadcrumbs and spray them with a bit of olive spray.
7. Place in the Air Fryer for ten to twelve minutes.

Chapter 6: Other Tasty Meats – Sides & Veggies

Variety Meals

Hot Dogs

Yields: 2 Servings

Ingredients:

2 hot dogs
2 buns for the hot dogs
2 tbsp. grated cheese

How to Prepare:

1. Allow the Air Fryer to warm up for four minutes at 390°F.
2. Arrange the hot dogs in the fryer and cook for five minutes or until done.
3. Transfer from the cooker to the bun and garnish with cheese.
4. Place the prepared dog in the fryer for about two minutes to melt the cheese.

Stromboli

Yields: 4 Servings

Ingredients:

1 pkg. (12-oz.) refrigerated pizza crust
¾ c. Mozzarella shredded cheese
3 c. shredded cheddar cheese
1 tbsp. milk
1 egg yolk
1/3 lb. sliced cooked ham
3 oz. roasted red bell peppers

How to Prepare:

1. Warm up the Air Fryer at 360°F.
2. Roll the dough until it is around ¼-inch thick.
3. Layer in the peppers, ham, and cheese on one side of the dough and fold to seal.
4. Combine the milk and eggs to brush the dough.
5. Put the Stromboli in the basket and set the timer for 15 minutes. Check it every five minutes or so—flip the Stromboli to the other side for thorough cooking.

Lamb

Lamb Meatballs

Yields: 4 Servings

Ingredients:

1 egg white
1 lb. ground lamb
4 oz. turkey
½ t. salt
2 minced garlic cloves
2 tbsp. parsley
1 tbsp. of each - chopped:
 -Coriander
 -Mint
1 tbsp. olive oil

How to Prepare:

1. Heat the Air Fryer to 320°F.
2. Combine all of the fixings in a mixing container. Blend well and shape into small meatballs.
3. Arrange in the Air Fryer and prepare for 15 minutes.
4. When ready pair it up with your favorite sauce or side dish; just remember to count those carbs.

Roasted Rack of Lamb with a Macadamia Crust

Ingredients:

1 clove of garlic
1 tbsp. olive oil
To Taste: Pepper and salt
1 ¾ lb. rack of lamb

Ingredients for the Crust:

3 oz. Macadamia nuts - unsalted
1 tbsp. each
 -Fresh rosemary
 -Breadcrumbs
1 egg

How to Prepare:

1. Preheat the Air Fryer to 220°F.
2. Chop the garlic clove into tiny bits. Make the garlic oil by combining the garlic and oil. Brush the lamb and flavor with salt and pepper.
3. Chop the nuts to a fine consistency in a bowl and blend in the rosemary and breadcrumbs. Beat/whip the egg in another dish.
4. Dredge the meat through the egg mixture and coat with the macadamia crust topping.
5. Place the rack of lamb in the Air Fryer basket—setting the timer for 30 minutes.
6. After the time is lapsed, raise the heat to 390°F—setting the time for an additional five minutes.
7. Take the meat from the fryer and let it rest for about ten minutes covered with some aluminum foil.

Substitutes to Consider: You can use cashews, hazelnuts, pistachios, or almonds if you would like a change of pace.

Veggies

Avocado Fries

Yields: 2 Servings

Ingredients:

1 large avocado
½ c. breadcrumbs
1 egg
½ t. salt

How to Prepare:

1. Set the Air Fryer to 390°F. Peel, remove the pit, and slice the avocado.
2. Prepare 2 shallow dishes, one with the breadcrumbs, and salt; and one with a beaten egg.
3. First, dip the avocado into the egg – then the breadcrumbs.
4. Add to the fryer for 10 minutes.
5. Serve anytime you want a delicious side dish or an appetizer.

Avocado Bacon Fries

Yields: 2 Servings

Ingredients:

1 egg
1 c. almond flour
4 strips bacon – cooked – small bits
2 large avocados – lengthwise cuts
For Frying: Olive oil

How to Prepare:

1. Set the temperature in the fryer to 355°F.
2. Whisk the eggs in one container. Add the flour with the bacon in another.
3. Slice the avocado and dip into the eggs then the flour mixture.
4. Drizzle oil in the fryer tray and air fry 10 minutes per side or until they're the way you like them.

Baked Potatoes

Yields: 3 Servings

Ingredients:

3 Russet or Idaho baking potatoes
1 tbsp. of each:
-Garlic
-Salt
1 t. parsley
1-2 tbsp. olive oil

How to Prepare:

1. Wash the potatoes and use a fork to punch holes in each one.
2. Oil and sprinkle the potatoes with the seasonings.
3. Add them to the fryer basket and air fry for 35-40 minutes.
4. Garnish with some sour cream and fresh parsley.

Blossoming Onion

Yields: 4 Servings

Ingredients:

4 small/2 med. onions
4 dollops of butter
1 tbsp. olive oil

How to Prepare:

1. Peel the skin from the onion and cut away the top and bottom to reveal flat ends.
2. Soak the onions in salt water for four hours to take away the harshness.
3. You will need to cut the onion as far down as you can without severing the onion body. Cut four times to make eight segments.
4. Preheat the fryer to 350°F.
5. Put the onions in the fryer and drizzle with the oil—placing a dollop of butter on each one.
6. Cook in the fryer until the outside is dark, usually about thirty minutes.

Serving Note: 4 dollops = 4 heaping tbsp.

Broccoli

Yields: 2-4 Servings

Ingredients:

2 lbs. broccoli crowns
2 tbsp. olive oil
1 t. kosher salt
½ t. black pepper
2 t. grated lemon zest
1/3 c. Kalamata olives
¼ c. shaved parmesan cheese

How to Prepare:

1. Cut the stems from the broccoli and slice them into 1 to 1-1/2- inch florets. Pit and cut the olives in half.
2. Over high heat, fill a medium pan with six cups of water—bring it to boiling. Toss in the florets and cook for three to four minutes. Remove and drain. Add the pepper, salt, and oil.
3. Set the AF to 400°F. Place the broccoli into the basket, close the drawer, and click the timer for 15 minutes. Toss/flip at seven minutes for even browning. When done, place the broccoli in the bowl.
4. Garnish with lemon zest, olives, and cheese. Enjoy immediately.

Brussels Sprouts

Yields: 4-5 Servings or approx. 1 pound

Ingredients:

5 t. olive oil
1 lb. fresh brussels sprouts
½ t. kosher salt

How to Prepare:

1. Prep the Vegetables: Trim the stems and remove any damaged outer leaves. Cut into halves, rinse, and dry. Toss with the oil and salt.
2. Set the AF temperature in advance to 390°F. Add the sprouts into the basket and cook for 15 minutes.
3. Shake the basket to make sure they cook evenly.

Buffalo Cauliflower

Yields: 4 Servings

Ingredients:

1 c. breadcrumbs
4 c. cauliflower florets
¼ c. each of:
-Buffalo sauce
-Melted butter
For the Dip: A favorite dressing

How to Prepare:

1. Place the butter in a microwaveable dish. Remove and whisk in the buffalo sauce.
2. Dip each of the florets in the butter mixture. The stem does not need to have sauce. Use the stem as a handle, hold it over a cup, and let the excess drip away.
3. Run the floret through the breadcrumbs to your liking. Drop them into the fryer. Cook for 14 to 17 minutes at 350°F. (The unit will not need to preheat since it is calculated into the time.)
4. You can shake the basket several times to be sure it is evenly browning. Enjoy with your favorite dip but be sure to eat it right away because the crunchiness goes away quickly.

Cooking Note: Reheat in the oven. Don't use the microwave or it will be mushy.

Button Mushroom Melt

Yields: 10 Mushrooms

Ingredients:

10 Button mushrooms
Italian dried mixed herbs
Salt and pepper
Mozzarella cheese
Cheddar cheese
Optional Garnish: Dried dill

How to Prepare:

1. Wash the mushrooms, remove the stems, and let drain.
2. Flavor with a pinch of black pepper, salt, herbs, and olive oil.
3. Heat the Air Fryer ahead of time to 356°F. (About three to five minutes should be okay.)
4. Add the mushrooms to the basket with the hollow section facing you. Sprinkle the cheese on top of each of the caps.
5. Add the mushrooms to the cooker for seven to eight minutes.
6. Serve piping hot with a drizzle of basil or other herbs.

Cauliflower Rice

Yields: 3 Servings

Ingredients for Round 1:

1 c. diced carrots (1½-2 carrots)
½ block extra firm or firm tofu
½ c. diced onions
2 tbsp. reduced sodium soy sauce

Ingredients for Round 2:

3 c. riced cauliflower
½ c. of each:
-Finely chopped broccoli
-Frozen peas
2 minced garlic cloves
1½ t. toasted sesame oil – optional
1 tbsp. of each:
  - Rice vinegar
  -Minced ginger
2 tbsp. reduced sodium soy sauce

How to Prepare:

1. Preheat the air fryer to 370°F.
2. Prepare the Cauliflower: Mince it into small pieces with a food processor or by hand with a box-style grater. You can also purchase the rice in the ready-made form.
3. Crumble the tofu (scrambled egg size) and add the remainder of the round one fixings. Air fry for ten minutes, shaking once.

4. Combine the round two ingredients in a large mixing container. Toss in with the fixings in the fryer. Air fry for another two to five minutes.

5. Check and shake every two minutes until done.

Charred Shishito Peppers

Yields: 4 Servings

Ingredients:

1 t. olive oil
1 juiced lemon
20 Shishito peppers
Sea salt to taste

How to Prepare:

1. Warm up the fryer to 390°F.
2. Toss the peppers with the oil and salt. Add them to the basket and cook 5 minutes.
3. Place on a platter with a squeeze of lemon. Serve and enjoy.

Garlic & Thyme Tomatoes

Yields: 4 Servings

Ingredients:

1 tbsp. olive oil
4 Roma tomatoes
1 minced clove of garlic
½ t. dried thyme
Freshly cracked black pepper
Salt

How to Prepare:

1. Warm up the fryer to 390°F.
2. Slice the tomatoes and remove the pithy parts and seeds. Toss them into a mixing container along with the pepper, salt, thyme, olive oil, and garlic.
3. Arrange them in the fryer with the cut side up. Air fry for 15 minutes.
4. Let them cool off a few minutes. Add on top of pasta, poultry, fish, or any meats.

Grilled Corn

Yields: 2-4 Servings

Ingredients:

2-3 small limes
2 t. paprika
2 - corn on the cob
Olive oil
½ c. grated feta cheese

How to Prepare:

1. Discard the corn silks and husks. Rub the corn thoroughly with the oil and sprinkle with some paprika.
2. Heat up the fryer to 392°F.
3. Place the corn into the basket. Set the timer for 12-15 minutes. Lower the time as needed if it is cooking too fast. Remove the corn from the fryer when done.
4. Grate some frozen feta cheese over the corn and drizzle with some lime juice.

Grilled Tomatoes

Yields: 2 Servings

Ingredients:

2 tomatoes
Cooking spray
Pepper
Herbs

How to Prepare:

1. Preheat the fryer to 320°F.
2. Wash and cut the tomatoes into halves. Spray each of them lightly with some cooking spray and place them cut side facing upwards. Sprinkle with your favorite spices—fresh or dried—including the pepper, sage, rosemary, basil, oregano, and any others of your choice.
3. Put them into the basket for 20 minutes or until they are to the doneness you want to achieve. Enjoy if they are ready—if not—cook for a few more minutes.

Honey Roasted Carrots

Yield: 4 Servings

Ingredients:

3 c. carrots
1 tbsp. of each:
-Honey
-Olive oil
To Taste: Salt and pepper

How to Prepare:

1. Cut the carrots into small chunks or use some baby carrots.
2. Combine the oil, honey, and carrots in a mixing dish, making sure they are thoroughly coated.
3. Sprinkle with some pepper and salt.
4. Arrange the carrots in the Air Fryer and cook at 392°F for 12 minutes.

Mediterranean Veggies

Yields: 4 Servings

Ingredients:

¼ c. cherry tomatoes
1 med. carrot
1 green pepper
1 large of each:
 -Parsnip
 -Cucumber
2 tbsp. of each:
-Garlic puree
-Honey
6 tbsp. olive oil
1 t. mixed herbs
To Taste: Pepper and salt

How to Prepare

1. Chop the cucumber and green pepper and add it to the bottom of the air fryer.
2. Peel and dice the carrot and parsnip, adding the whole cherry tomatoes.
3. Drizzle with three tablespoons of oil and cook at 356°F for 15 minutes.
4. Mix the rest of the ingredients in an 'air fryer safe' baking dish.
5. Add the veggies to the marinade and shake well. Give it a sprinkle of pepper and salt and cook at 392°F for another five minutes.
   a. *Note*: You can substitute and experiment with different veggies, but don't use the cucumber and

cauliflower in the same dish. Together, they produce too much liquid.

6. Serve and enjoy. You can also add some honey and sweet potatoes to the mixture.

Onion Rings

Yields: 2 Servings

Ingredients:

1 large onion – approx. 14 oz.
¼ c. egg whites
¼ t. salt
2/3 c. whole-wheat panko breadcrumbs
1 t. of each:
-Garlic powder
-Onion powder
2 tbsp. whole-wheat flour
1/8 t. black pepper

How to Prepare:

1. Cut away the ends and the outer layer of the onion. Slice into 1/-inch slices and separate them into rings.
2. Whisk the egg whites in a small dish.
3. Combine the seasonings and breadcrumbs in another bowl.
4. Add some flour and the rings into a plastic bag and shake to cover the rings evenly. Coat them with the egg whites and the breadcrumb mixture.
5. Add the coated rings to the air fryer at 392°F.
6. Bake for about six minutes or to your liking.

Parmesan Truffle Oil Fries

Yields: 6 Servings

Ingredients:

1 tbsp of each:
-Olive oil
-Canola oil
3 large russet potatoes
2 tbsp. of each:
-White truffle oil
-Shredded parmesan cheese
1 tbsp. chopped parsley
Salt and Pepper to your taste

How to Prepare:

1. Warm the fryer to 380°F.
2. Peel the potatoes and cut lengthwise. Add to a bowl of water to soak for a minimum of thirty minutes (one hour is better.) Add them to a baking pan and coat them with the olive oil, canola oil, and one tablespoon of the white truffle oil. Toss in the seasonings.
3. Prepare two batches. Cook for 15-20 minutes. Shake at the ten-minute intervals. Remove the first batch and add the remainder of the potatoes.
4. Transfer them to the baking tray, sprinkle the rest of the oil, and add the parmesan cheese to the fries. Top with the parsley and enjoy.

Potato Hash

Yields: 4 Cups

Ingredients:

1.65 lbs. potatoes
½ of a green pepper
2 t. duck fat/olive oil
1 med. onion
½ t. of each:
-Thyme
-Black pepper
1 t. salt substitute
1 c. egg substitute
Cooking spray

How to Prepare:

1. Melt the fat of choice in the bucket for two minutes.
2. Prep the Veggies: Chop the onion and the deseeded green pepper. Toss them into the Air Fryer and cook for five minutes.
3. Prepare the potatoes into small cubes and add them to the fryer with the seasonings. Cook for 30 minutes.
4. Lightly spray a skillet with the cooking spray. Crack some of the pepper into the pan – heating a minute or so. Break the egg and cook until done. Chop and add the egg to the air fryer and cook another five minutes.
5. Serve hot and garnish, as you like. A tomato would be delicious.

Roasted Veggie Pasta Salad

Yields: 6-8 Servings

Ingredients:

4 oz. brown mushrooms
1 red onion
1 yellow squash
1 zucchini
1 each bell peppers
 -Red
 -Green
 -Orange
Pinch of Fresh ground pepper and salt
1 t. Italian seasoning
1 c. grape tomatoes
½ c. pitted Kalamata olives
1 lb. cooked Rigatoni or Penne Rigate
¼ c. olive oil
2 tbsp. fresh chopped basil
3 tbsp. balsamic vinegar

How to Prepare:

1. Cut the squash and zucchini into half-moons. Cut the peppers into large chunks and slice the red onion. Slice the tomatoes and olives in half.
2. Preheat the Air Fryer to 380°F.
3. Put the mushrooms, peppers, red onion, squash, and zucchini in a large container. Drizzle with some of the oil—tossing well. Sprinkle in the pepper, salt, and Italian seasoning.

4. Place in the Air Fryer until the veggies are soft (not mushy), usually about for 12 to 15 minutes. For even roasting, shake the basket about halfway through the cooking cycle.

5. Combine the roasted veggies, olives, cooked pasta, and tomatoes, in a large container; mix well. Add the vinegar, and toss. (Use as little oil as possible, just enough to coat the vegetables.)

6. Keep it refrigerated until ready to serve—adding the fresh basil for last.

Skinny Fries

Yields: 2 Servings

Ingredients:

Salt
2-3 t. vegetable or olive oil
2-3 russet potatoes

How to Prepare:

1. Slice the potatoes into ¼-inch segments. Use a mandolin with a julienne blade.
2. Rinse the potatoes several times under cold water. Soak them overnight or a minimum of ten minutes.
3. Set the temperature to the fryer at 380°F. Prepare two batches.
4. Air fry for 15 minutes (shake once or twice). Toss in the first batch to reheat a minute or so.
5. Arrange on a plate and flavor with some more salt. Serve with your choice of garnishes.

Stuffed Mushrooms

Yields: 3 Servings

Ingredients:

3 Portobello mushrooms
1 t. minced garlic
1 med. diced onion
3 tbsp. grated mozzarella cheese
1 tbsp. olive oil
2 slices chopped ham
1 diced tomato
1 diced green pepper
½ t. sea salt
¼ t. pepper

How to Prepare:

1. Warm up the Air Fryer to 320°F.
2. Wash, dry, and remove the stems from the mushrooms. Drizzle with oil and set aside for now.
3. Combine the pepper, salt, cheese, tomato, onion, garlic, bell peppers, and ham; stuff into the mushroom caps.
4. Add the mushrooms to the fryer for 8 minutes.
5. Serve with your favorite entrée.

Twice Baked Loaded Air-Fried Potatoes

Yields: 2 Servings

Ingredients:

1 t. olive oil
1 potato – 14-16 oz.
1 tbsp. each of:
-Finely chopped green onion
-Unsalted butter
2 tbsp. heavy cream
1/8 t. black pepper
¼ t. salt

How to Prepare:

1. Cook the bacon about ten minutes - reserving the fat - and chop into ½-inch pieces.
2. Finely chop the onions.
3. Coat the potato with the oil and add to the AF basket. Set the temperature to 400°F for 30 minutes. Add a little more oil to the fryer, turn the potato, and cook for another 30 minutes. Let it cool off for a minimum of 20 minutes.
4. When cooled, slice the potato lengthways. Scoop out the pulp leaving about ¼-inch borders to support the filling.
5. Whisk together the scooped potato along with the bacon fat, bacon bits, ¼ cup of the cheese, 1 ½ tsp of the onions, pepper, salt, butter, and lastly the cream. Combine well.
6. Scoop the mixture into the prepared skins. Garnish with the cheese and place them in the Air Fryer.

7. Set the timer for 20 minutes or until the tops are browned, and the cheese are melted.
8. Sprinkle the rest of the onions on top of the potato and serve.

Sides

Bread Choices

Bread Rolls with Potato Stuffing

Yields: 4 Servings

Ingredients:

8 slices bread (white part only)
5 large potatoes
1 small bunch finely chopped coriander
2 seeded and finely chopped green chilies
½ t. turmeric
2 curry leaf sprigs
½ t. mustard seeds
2 finely chopped small onions
2 tbsp. oil (frying and brushing)
Salt if desired

How to Prepare:

1. Warm up the Air Fryer to 392°F. Cut away the edges of the bread.
2. Peel the potatoes, and boil. Use one teaspoon of salt and mash the potatoes.
3. In the meantime, on the stovetop, use a skillet to combine the mustard seeds and one teaspoon of the oil. Add the onions when the seeds sputter, continue frying until they become translucent. Toss in the curry and turmeric.
4. Fry the mixture a few seconds, add the salt, and mashed potatoes. Mix well and let it cool. Shape eight portions of the dough into an oval shape. Set them to the side.

5. Wet the bread with water and press it into your palm to remove the excess water. Place the oval potato into the bread and roll it around the potato mixture. Be sure they are completely sealed.

6. Brush the basket and the potato rolls with oil and set to the side. Set the Air Fryer timer for 12 to 13 minutes. Let them cook until crispy and browned.

Buttermilk Biscuits

Yields: 2 Servings

Ingredients:

½ c. cake flour
¾ tsp. salt
¼ tsp. baking soda
1-¼ c. all-purpose flour
1 t. granulated sugar
½ t. baking powder
¾ c. buttermilk
4 tbsp. unsalted cold butter (cut into cubes) + melted 1 tbsp.

Optional for Serving:

Honey or preserves
Butter

Preparation Note: Additional flour is needed for dusting the counter or cutting board.

How to Prepare:

1. Program the Air Fryer to 400°F.
2. Sift together the all-purpose flour, sugar, baking soda, cake flour, and the salt in a medium mixing dish.
3. Use a pastry cutter (or your fingers) to blend the ingredients into pea-sized consistency. Pour in the buttermilk, stir using a rubber spatula (or your hands), and make a dough ball. Try not to over-mix the dough.

4. Sprinkle some flour on the counter surface and begin to press the dough into about a ½-inch thickness. It should be approximately eight inches in diameter.

5. Use a cutter to cut the dough into biscuits. Dip the tip of the cutter with the flour making a swift cut. Don't twist the dough because it could prevent it from rising.

6. Arrange the biscuits in a pan and brush them with the melted butter. Place the dough in the basket of the fryer and set the timer for eight minutes. Enjoy the finished product with some honey or your favorite preserves, jam, or jelly.

Cheesy Garlic Bread

Yields: 3-4 Servings

Ingredients:

5 round bread slices
5 t. sun-dried tomato pesto
3 chopped garlic cloves
4 tbsp. melted butter
1 c. grated Mozzarella cheese

Garnish Options:

Chili flakes
Chopped basil leaves
Oregano

How to Prepare:

1. Preheat the Air Fryer to 356°F.
2. Cut the loaf of bread into five thick slices.
3. Add the butter, pesto, and cheese onto the bread.
4. Put the slices in the preheated cooker for six to eight minutes.
5. Garnish with your choice of toppings.

Note: Round or Baguette bread was used for this recipe. It is recommended to add the finely chopped garlic cloves to the melted butter ahead of time for the best results.

Garlic Knots

Yields: 4 Servings

Ingredients:

Marinara sauce
1 t. sea salt
1 lb. frozen pizza crust dough
1 tbsp. each:
 -Garlic powder
 -Grated Parmesan cheese
 -Fresh chopped parsley

How to Prepare:

1. Program the Air Fryer to 360°F.
2. Roll out the dough until it is about 1 ½ to 2-inches thick. Slice it approximately ¾-inches apart—lengthwise.
3. Roll the dough and make it into knots.
4. Add the cheese, oil, and spices in a bowl, and roll each knot in the mixture before placing it into the fry basket.
5. Set the timer for 12 minutes and flip the knots halfway through the cooking process (six minutes).
6. Serve with a dish of marinara sauce.

Phyllo Pastry

Yields: 12 phyllo sheet layers

Ingredients:

1 t. salt
4 c. flour
1 1/3 c. tepid water
¼ c. olive oil

How to Prepare:

1. Sift the salt and flour and add the water and oil.
2. Combine to make a soft dough. Knead for about ten minutes.
3. When done, wrap the dough in some plastic wrap to rest about one hour at room temperature.
4. Shape 12 balls out of the dough. Cover the dough and shape each of the balls into a six-inch square.
5. Dust them with flour and roll them onto a dowel. Unroll them and coat with flour. They will remain usable for about one week.

Chapter 7: Snacks & Appetizers

Now for the tasty treats!

Apple Chips

Yields: 6-8 Servings

Ingredients:

1 tbsp. olive oil
6 large red apples
1 pinch of cinnamon

How to Prepare:

1. Preheat the fryer to 356°F.
2. Cut the apple lengthwise and add them to the Air Fryer with a teaspoon of the oil.
3. Cook them until they are crispy or around ten minutes.
4. Add the cinnamon, give them a toss, and enjoy.

Bacon-Wrapped Chicken

Yields: 3 Servings

Ingredients:

1 breast of chicken
6 strips unsmoked bacon
1 tbsp. soft garlic cheese

How to Prepare:

1. Slice the chicken into six pieces.
2. Spread the garlic cheese over each bacon strip. Add a piece of chicken to each one. Roll and secure with a toothpick.
3. Prepare the Air Fryer a couple of minutes. Add the wraps and cook 15 minutes.

Bacon-Wrapped Prawns

Yields: 4 Servings

Ingredients:

1 lb. of each:
 -Bacon slices
 -Peeled prawns

How to Prepare:

1. Warm up the Air Fryer to 390°F.
2. Wrap a bacon slice around each prawn and add to the fryer basket
3. Prepare for five minutes and enjoy.

Bacon-Wrapped Tater Tots

Yields: 4 Servings

Ingredients:

3 tbsp. sour cream
1 lb. sliced bacon - medium
1 large bag crispy tater tots
4 scallions
½ c. shredded cheddar cheese

How to Prepare:

1. Warm up the Air Fryer to 400°F.
2. Wrap each of the tots in bacon and place them into the fryer basket. Don't overcrowd, keep them in a single layer.
3. Set the AF timer for 8 minutes.
4. When the timer beeps, place the tots on a plate.
5. Serve with the scallions and cheese garnish. Add a dash of sour cream and enjoy.

Cajun Spiced Snack Mix

Yields: 10 Cups

Ingredients for the Mix:

2 tbsp. Cajun or Creole seasoning
½ c. melted butter
2 c. of each:
-Mini pretzels
-Peanuts
-Mini wheat thin crackers
4 c. plain popcorn

Ingredients for the Cajun Seasoning:

1 t. of each:
-Paprika
-Garlic
-Cayenne pepper
-Black pepper
2 t. salt
½ t. of each:
-Onion powder
-Thyme
-Oregano

How to Prepare:

1. Heat the Air Fryer in advance to 370°F.
2. Mix the Cajun seasoning and melted butter.
3. In a larger container, combine the popcorn, pretzels, crackers, and peanuts. Empty the butter over the snack and toss.

4. Make two batches. Add half of the ingredients into the Air Fryer for eight to ten minutes. Toss during the process for even cooking.
5. Cool on a cookie sheet. Store in an airtight container.

Cheese Balls

Yields: 5 Servings

Ingredients:

1 egg
8 oz. pkg. mozzarella balls
½ c. of each:
 -Coconut flakes
 -Almond flour
To Taste:
 -Thyme
-Pepper
 -Paprika

How to Prepare:

1. Program the Air Fryer to 400°F.
2. Whisk the egg in one bowl and combine the spices with flour in a separate bowl.
3. Sprinkle the balls with the coconut flakes and the flour.
4. Freeze the cheese balls for 5 minutes. Add to the fryer for 3 minutes and enjoy!

Cheese & Onion Nuggets

Yields: 4 Servings

Ingredients:

1 egg
7 oz. grated Edam cheese
2 diced spring onions
Salt and pepper – as desired
1 tbsp. of each:
 -Dried thyme
 -Coconut oil

How to Prepare:

1. Program the frying unit to 350°F.
2. Combine all of the fixings (omit the cheese).
3. Make 8 balls out of the mixture and stuff the cheese in the center. Place in the fridge 1 hr.
4. Whisk the egg and use a pastry brush to coat the nuggets. Place in the Air Fryer for 12 minutes.
5. Enjoy anytime.

Chickpeas with Ranch Seasoning

Yields: 4 Servings

Ingredients:

2 tbsp. olive oil – divided
1 can – 15 oz. chickpeas
1 t. sea salt
1 batch homemade ranch seasoning
2 tbsp. lemon juice

How to Prepare:

1. Preheat the fryer to 400°F.
2. Drain but don't rinse the chickpeas and add them to a bowl with one tablespoon of the olive oil and air fry for 15 minutes.
3. Add the chickpeas back into the dish and toss in the rest of the oil, salt, seasoning, and lemon juice.
4. Add back to the fryer at 350°F for another five minutes
5. Serve, store, and enjoy. You can store them on the counter for a couple of days.

Crispy Corn Tortilla Chips

Yields: 1 Serving

Ingredients:

8 corn tortillas
1 tbsp. olive oil
Salt if desired

How to Prepare:

1. Program the AF to 392°F.
2. Use a sharp knife to cut the tortillas. Brush each tortilla with oil.
3. Air fry two batches for three minutes each. Sprinkle with a pinch of salt.

Feta Triangles

Yields: 4 Servings

Ingredients:

4 oz. feta cheese
1 egg yolk
2 tbsp. flat-leafed parsley
2 sheets phyllo pastry
2 tbsp. olive oil
To Taste: Ground black pepper
1 finely chopped scallion

How to Prepare:

1. Finely chop the parsley.
2. Program the heat in the Air Fryer to 390°F.
3. Whisk the egg and blend in the scallion, feta, and parsley. Cut the dough into three strips.
4. Place a heaping teaspoon of the feta mix underneath the pastry strip.
5. Fold the tip to form a triangle as you work your way around the strip.
6. Use a small amount of oil and brush each of the triangles before placing them in the cooker basket cooking them for three minutes.
7. Lower the heat to 360°F and continue cooking for an additional two minutes.

Fried Pickles

Yields: 14 Pickles

Ingredients:

¼ c. all-purpose flour
1/8 t. baking powder
14 thinly sliced dill pickles – refrigerated & crunchy
Pinch of salt
3 tbsp. dark beer (German beer - if vegan)
2-3 tbsp. water
6 tbsp. panko breadcrumbs
2 tbsp. cornstarch
Pinch of cayenne pepper
½ t. paprika
For Frying: Organic canola or oil spray
¼-1/2 cup ranch dressing

How to Prepare:

1. Use paper towels to dry the pickles. Set to the side for later.
2. Mix the beer, two tablespoons of water, a pinch of salt, baking powder, and flour. Its consistency should be similar to waffle batter.
3. Prepare two platters. One will have the cornstarch, and the other will have a pinch of salt, the cayenne, paprika, and breadcrumbs.
4. Bread the pickles. Prepare the working surface with the pickles, cornstarch, beer batter, and panko mixture.
5. Dip each of the pickles into the cornstarch and remove excess starch. Dip each one into the batter until evenly covered. Let the excess batter drip away. Lastly, add the

pickle into the panko mixture to adequately cover all surfaces.

6. Add the finished pickles to the air fryer basket. Heat the fryer to 360°F.

7. Do this in batches, spraying each layer with some cooking oil. Check the pickles after eight minutes. If not ready, add them back and cook checking every minute.

8. Serve with the ranch dressing and enjoy!

Garlic Roasted Almonds

Yields: 8 Servings

Ingredients:

2 c. raw almonds
¼ t. paprika
1 t. paprika
1 tbsp. of each:
-Garlic powder
-Soy sauce

How to Prepare:

1. Heat the fryer to 320°F.
2. Stir everything together, (omit the almonds for now), to form a thick paste.
3. Now, add the almonds. After they are well coated, toss them into the fryer basket to cook for six to eight minutes.
4. Check every two or three minutes to prevent the almonds from sticking. After six minutes, check every minute. They are done when the inside is also crunchy.
5. Cool for 10-15 minutes and add to a storage container. They are great for 2-3 days for the best flavor results.

Grilled Cheese Sandwich

Yields: 2 Servings

Ingredients:

½ c. sharp cheddar cheese
4 slices white bread or brioche
¼ c. melted butter

How to Prepare:

1. Program the Air Fryer temperature to 360°F.
2. Spread butter on each side of all of the bread slices and add the cheese on two of them. Put them together.
3. Cook until browned, about five to seven minutes.

Kale Chips

Yields: 2 Servings

Ingredients:

1 head cabbage
1 tbsp. olive oil
1 t. soy sauce

How to Prepare:

1. Rinse the kale, dry, and add to a mixing bowl with the rest of the fixings.
2. Set the fryer at 200°F and add the kale. Toss ½ way through the cycle.
3. Serve anytime.

Mac "N" Cheese Balls

Yields: 2 Servings

Ingredients:

2 c. macaroni and cheese – leftovers are good to use
1/3 c. shredded cheddar cheese
3 eggs
2 c. milk
¾ c. white flour
1 c. plain breadcrumbs

How to Prepare:

1. Warm up the Air Fryer to 360°F.
2. Combine the leftovers with the shredded cheese.
3. Put the breadcrumbs into a dish.
4. Measure the flour into another bowl.
5. Combine the milk and eggs.
6. Make a ping-pong sized ball from the mac "n" cheese.
7. Roll the balls in the flour, eggs, and lastly the breadcrumbs.
8. Arrange the balls in the fryer basket. Press 'M' and go to the chicken icon.
9. Program the timer for ten minutes – rotating halfway through the cooking cycle. Scoop out and enjoy.

Mini Bacon Wrapped Burritos – Vegan

Yields: 4 Mini Burritos

Ingredients:

2 servings Tofu Scramble or Vegan Egg
2-3 tbsp. tamari
2 tbsp. cashew butter
1-2 tbsp. of each:
 -Water
 -Liquid smoke
4 pieces of rice paper

Vegetable Add-Ins:

8 strips roasted red pepper
1/3 cup sweet potato roasted cubes
1 small sautéed tree broccoli
A handful of greens (kale, spinach, etc.)
6-8 stalks of fresh asparagus

How to Prepare:

1. Line the pan used for baking with parchment. Preheat the Air Fryer to 350°F.
2. Whisk the tamari, cashew butter, water, and liquid smoke; set to the side.
3. Prepare the fillings.
4. Hold a rice paper under fresh running water—getting both sides wet—just a second. Place on the plate to fill.
5. Start by filling the ingredients –just-off- from the center—leaving the sides of the paper free.

6. Fold in two of the sides as you would when you make a burrito. Seal them and dip each one in the liquid smoke mixture—coating completely.

7. Cook until crispy, usually about eight to ten minutes.

Mini Quiche Wedges

Yields: 9 Servings

Ingredients:

1 (3 ½ oz.) homemade pizza crust or store-bought
1 egg
(1.4 oz.) grated cheese
½ tbsp. oil
3 tbsp. whipping cream
Fresh ground pepper
2 small pie molds

How to Prepare:

1. Program the heat setting on the Air Fryer to 392°F.
2. Use a bit of cooking spray to grease the molds. Line them with the dough pressing down around the edges.
3. Whisk the cheese, cream, and egg flavoring with some pepper and salt to taste. Empty the mixture into the molds.
4. Put the mold into the basket and set the timer for 12 minutes. Bake the second one the same way.
5. Take them from the molds and slice each of the quiches into six wedges.
6. You can serve at room temperature or warm.

Mozzarella Sticks

Yields: 4 Servings

Ingredients:

2 eggs
1 lb./1 block mozzarella cheese
1 c. plain breadcrumbs
¼ c. white flour
3 tbsp. nonfat milk

How to Prepare:

1. Preheat the fryer to 400°F.
2. Slice the cheese into ½-inch x 3-inch sticks.
3. Whisk the milk and egg together in one bowl, with the oil and breadcrumbs in individual dishes as well.
4. Dredge the sliced cheese through the oil, egg, and breadcrumbs.
5. Place the sticks on bread tin and put them in the freezer compartment for about an hour or two.
6. Arrange them in small increments (don't overcrowd) into the AF basket. Cook for 12 minutes.

Party Meatballs

Yields: 24 Servings

Ingredients:

2 ½ tbsp. Worcestershire sauce
1 lb. ground beef
1 tbsp. of each:
 - Tabasco sauce
 -Lemon juice
¾ c. tomato ketchup
¼ c. vinegar
½ t. dry mustard
½ c. brown sugar
3 crushed gingersnaps

How to Prepare:

1. Combine all of the seasonings in a large mixing container—blending well.
2. Mix the beef and continue churning the ingredients.
3. Make the balls and put them in the fryer. Cook on 375°F for 15 minutes.
4. They are ready when the center is done, and they're crispy.

5. Place them on the toothpicks before serving.

Pigs in a Blanket

Yields: 4 Servings

Ingredients:

1 can (8 oz.) crescent rolls
1 pkg. cocktail wieners (12 oz.)

How to Prepare:

1. Set the Air Fryer to 330°F.
2. Drain the franks and thoroughly dry them using two paper towels.
3. Slice the dough into strips of about 1 ½ inches x 1-inch (rectangular).
4. Roll the dough around the franks leaving the ends open. Put them in the freezer to firm up for about five minutes.
5. Take them out and arrange them in the AF for six to eight minutes. Adjust the temperature to 390°F and continue to cook for approximately three minutes.

Pita Bread Cheese Pizza

Yields: 1-2 Servings

Ingredients:

1 drizzle of extra-virgin olive oil
1 tbsp. pizza sauce
1- pita bread
¼ cup Mozzarella cheese
1 stainless steel short-legged trivet

Ingredients for the Toppings:

¼ c. sausage
7 pepperoni slices
½ t. fresh minced garlic
1 tbsp. thinly sliced onions

How to Prepare:

1. Heat the fryer to 350°F. Spoon the sauce onto the bread. Toss on the toppings and give it a drizzle of oil.
2. Arrange it in the Air Fryer and set the trivet over the bread.
3. Let it go for six minutes.

Potato Skin Wedges

Yields: 6 Servings

Ingredients:

6 med. russet potatoes
1 ½ t. paprika
2 tbsp. canola oil
½ t. of each:
-Salt
-Freshly cracked black pepper

How to Prepare:

1. Wash the potatoes and boil in salted water for forty minutes.
2. Place them in the fridge to chill for about thirty minutes. Quarter when they have cooled.
3. Whisk the salt, paprika, pepper, and oil in a mixing dish. Toss the potatoes into the mixture and arrange them into the cooking basket with the skin side down.
4. Cook them about 14 to 16 minutes.

Spiced Nuts

Yields: 3 Cups

Ingredients:

1 beaten egg white
¼ t. ground cloves
½ t. ground cinnamon
Pinch of cayenne pepper
Salt to your liking
1 c. of each:
 -Pecan halves
 -Cashews
 -Almonds

How to Prepare:

1. Mix the spices with the egg white.
2. Warm up the fryer to 300°F.
3. Toss the nuts into the mixture and shake.
4. Prepare in the Air Fryer for 25 minutes; stirring several times.
5. Enjoy every morsel!

Sweet & Salty Snack Mix

Yields: 10 Cups

Ingredients:

3 tbsp. melted butter
½ c. honey
1 t. salt
1 c. of each:
-Pumpkin seeds
-Cashews
2 c. of each:
-Sesame sticks
-Granola
-Mini pretzels
-Crispy corn puffs – ex. Corn Pops®

How to Prepare:

1. Combine the butter, honey, and salt – stirring well.
2. In a large container, add the puff cereal, pretzels, pumpkin seeds, granola, cashews, and sesame sticks. Pour the honey mixture and toss until well combined.
3. Set the temperature of the fryer to 370°F.
4. It will take two batches. Air fry for 10-12 minutes until the treats are lightly browned. Be sure to toss the basket to allow them to cook throughout and not burn on the tops.
5. Let the mixture cool on a baking tray, and store for up to a week in an airtight container. What a perfect gift!

Zucchini Roll-Ups

Yields: 2 Servings

Ingredients:

1 c. goat cheese
3 zucchinis
Sea salt to taste
¼ t. black pepper
1 tbsp. olive oil

How to Prepare:

1. Program the Air Fryer to 390°F.
2. Slice the zucchini thin – lengthwise. Brush each strip with the oil.
3. Mix the cheese with the salt and pepper. Scoop onto the zucchini strips, roll, and fasten with a toothpick.
4. Arrange in the fryer and prepare for 5 minutes. Yummy!

Chapter 8: Desserts

Air Fried Plantains

Yields: 4 Servings

Ingredients:

2 t. avocado or sunflower oil
2 ripened – almost brown – plantains
⅛ t. salt – optional

How to Prepare:

1. Warm up the fryer to 400°F.
2. Slice the plantains at an angle for a ½-inch thickness.
3. Combine the oil, salt, and plantains in a container – making sure you coat the surface thoroughly.
4. Air fry for eight to ten minutes; shake after five minutes. If they are not done to your liking, add a minute or two more making sure they don't burn.

Apple Fries with Caramel Cream Dip

Yields: 8-10 Servings

Ingredients:

3 apples – ex. Honey-crisp
3 beaten eggs
½ c. flour
¼ c. sugar
1 c. graham cracker crumbs
8 oz. whipped cream cheese
½ c. caramel sauce (+) more for garnish

How to Prepare:

1. Peel and slice the apples into eight wedges. In a large bowl, toss the flour and apple slices together.
2. Prepare a dish with the eggs. Mix the sugar and crackers in another bowl. Dip the apples in the egg and then the crumbs coating all sides. Arrange on a baking sheet.
3. Set the fryer to 380°F. Brush or spray the bottom of the fryer with oil.
4. Prepare in two batches by placing them in a single layer –spraying the batch lightly. Cook for five minutes, flip, and cook for another two minutes.
5. Make the cream dip by combining the caramel sauce and cream cheese.
6. Serve the hot apple fries with the caramel dip and enjoy.

Apricot & Blackberry Crumble

Yields: 6 Servings

Ingredients:

5 ½ oz. fresh blackberries
2 tbsp. lemon juice
18 oz. fresh apricots
½ c. sugar
Pinch of salt
1 c. flour
5 tbsp. cold butter

How to Prepare:

1. Heat the Air Fryer to 390°F.
2. Lightly grease an eight-inch oven dish with a small amount of cooking oil.
3. Remove the stones, cut the apricots into cubes, and put them in a container.
4. Combine the blackberries, lemon juice, and two tablespoons of sugar with the apricots and mix. Place the fruit in the oven dish.
5. Combine a pinch of salt, the remainder of the sugar, and the flour in a mixing container. Add one tablespoon cold water and the butter; using your fingertips to make a crumbly mixture.
6. Sprinkle the crumbles over the fruit and press down.
7. Place the dish into the basket and slide it into the Air Fryer for 20 minutes. It is ready when it is cooked thoroughly, and the top is browned.

Blackberry Pie

Yields: 8 Servings

Ingredients:

1 large egg
2 tbsp. unsalted butter
1 tbsp. baking powder
1 scoop stevia
1 c. almond flour
½ c. blackberries
Also Needed: Parchment paper

How to Prepare:

1. Heat up the Air Fryer to 350°F.
2. Whisk the egg and add the butter, stevia, and baking powder.
3. Reserve 1 t. of the flour and add the rest to the mixture. Knead until smooth – not sticky.
4. Cover the fryer basket with the paper and add the dough. Flatten into the shape of a piecrust and add the berries. Sprinkle with the rest of the almond flour on top.
5. Air fry until it's golden (20 min.) Chill before slicing to serve.

Cheesecake

Yields: 6 Servings

Ingredients:

½ c. almonds
6 tbsp. soft butter
1 tbsp. stevia
½ t. vanilla extract
1 c. cream cheese
2 eggs
2 tbsp. swerve
¼ t. cinnamon
1 t. lemon zest
Also Needed: Parchment paper

How to Prepare:

1. Combine the butter, vanilla, stevia, and sliced almonds.
2. Cover the Air Fryer tray with the paper and add the cheesecake crust (step 1).
3. Combine the cinnamon, swerve, lemon zest, and cream cheese.
4. Use a hand mixer to prepare the eggs until soft and fluffy. Pour the cream cheese mixture over the almond crust.
5. Set the Air Fryer temperature to 310°F. Cook for 16 minutes. When done, chill for at least 2 hours.
6. Then, slice and enjoy!

Cherry Pie

Yields: 8 Servings

Ingredients:

2 refrigerated pie crusts
1 can cherry pie filling (21 oz.)
1 tbsp. milk
1 egg yolk

How to Prepare:

1. Preheat the fryer to 310°F.
2. Stab holes into the crust after placing into a pie plate. Allow the excess to hang over the edges. Place in the AF for five minutes
3. Take the basket out and set the crust on the counter. Fill it with the cherries. Remove the excess crust.
4. Cut the remaining crust into ¾-inch strips placing them as a lattice across the pie.
5. Make an egg wash with the milk and egg. Lastly, brush the pie.
6. Bake for fifteen minutes. Serve with the ice cream of your choice.

Chocolate Chip Cookies

Yields: 5 Servings

Ingredients:

1 egg
2 tbsp. dark chocolate chips
3 tbsp. of each:
-Unsalted butter
-Crushed macadamia nuts
1 c. almond flour
½ t. vanilla extract
1 t. stevia
¼ t. of each:
-Baking powder
-Salt

How to Prepare:

1. Whisk the eggs and blend in the butter and flour.
2. Mix in the rest of the fixings and knead the dough.
3. Make 5 balls for the cookie dough.
4. Program the Air Fryer to 360°F. for a minute or so to warm up.
5. Arrange the cookies in the fryer and flatten (just a little) and cook for 15 minutes.
6. Cool slightly and enjoy. There is nothing like a piping hot cookie right out of the cooker!

Chocolate Soufflés

Yields: 2 Servings

Ingredients:

¼ c. butter
3 oz. semi-sweet chopped chocolate
2 separated eggs
½ t. pure vanilla extract
2 tbsp. all-purpose flour
3 tbsp. sugar Heavy cream for serving
Dusting: Powdered sugar
Also Needed: 2 ramekins

How to Prepare:

1. Apply some butter and sugar in the ramekins, shake, and dump out the excess of sugar.
2. Melt the butter and chocolate in a double boiler or microwave.
3. Combine the egg yolks (beating well). Blend in the sugar and vanilla, stir, and add the butter/chocolate mixture. Lastly, add the flour and mix until the lumps are gone.
4. Warm up the fryer to 330°F.
5. Whisk the egg whites to create soft peaks and gradually fold into the chocolate mixture.
6. Dump the batter slowly into the prepared ramekins. You need to leave a ½-inch space at the top. Arrange them in the basket of the fryer and cook for 14 minutes. It should be browned on the top. Dust with the sugar and enjoy. You can also add some heavy cream to pour over the soufflé at the table.

Donut Bread Pudding

Yields: 4 Servings

Ingredients:

6 glazed donuts
4 raw egg yolks
1 ½ c. whipping cream
¼ c. sugar
¾ c. frozen sweet cherries
1 t. cinnamon
½ c. of each:
 -Semi-sweet chocolate baking chips
 -Raisins

How to Prepare:

1. Preheat the fryer at 310°F.
2. Combine the wet ingredients in a container and combine the rest of the ingredients and mix.
3. Pour into a baking pan and cover it with foil. Place it into the basket and set the timer for 60 minutes.
4. Chill the bread pudding thoroughly before serving.

Green Avocado Pudding

Yields: 3 Servings

Ingredients:

1 pitted avocado
5 tbsp. almond milk
3 t. stevia
¼ t of each:
 -Vanilla extract
 -Salt
1 tbsp. cocoa powder

How to Prepare:

1. Warm up the Air Fryer a couple of minutes at 360°F.
2. Peel and mash the avocado and combine with the milk, salt, vanilla extract, and stevia. Stir in the cocoa powder.
3. Prepare in the Air Fryer for 3 minutes.
4. Chill well and serve.

Lemon Ricotta Cheesecake

Yields: 2 Servings

Ingredients:

1 lemon
2/3 c. sugar
2 c. ricotta
2 t. vanilla essence

How to Prepare:

1. Zest and juice the lemon.
2. Heat the Air Fryer to 320°F.
3. Mix the sugar, ricotta, one tablespoon lemon juice as well as the zest, and the vanilla essence—stirring until combined. Blend in the cornstarch and pour into the oven dish.
4. Place the dish in the Air Fryer basket and set the timer for 25 minutes.
5. The middle should be set when the cake is done.
6. Leave the cheesecake on a wire rack to cool before serving.

Marshmallow Peanut Butter Turnovers

Yields: 4 Servings

Ingredients:

4 defrosted sheets filo pastry/homemade
4 tbsp. chunky peanut butter
2 oz. melted butter
4 t. marshmallow fluff
Pinch of sea salt

How to Prepare:

1. Program the temperature of the Air Fryer to 360°F.
2. Use the melted butter to brush one sheet of the filo. Put the second sheet on top and brush it also with butter.
3. Continue the process until you have completed all four sheets. Cut the layers into four (4) 12-inch x 3-inch strips.
4. Place one teaspoon of the marshmallow fluff on the underside and one tablespoon of the peanut butter.
5. Fold the tip over the filo strip to form a triangle, making sure the filling is completely wrapped.
6. Seal the ends with a small amount of butter. Place the completed turnovers into the AF for three to five minutes.
7. When done, they will be fluffy and golden brown.
8. Add a touch of sea salt for the sweet/salty combo.

Special Notes: The Phyllo or Filo pastry is a little different than regular pastry. It is tissue thin and has minimal fat content. It is considered acceptable by some bakers and is interchange the filo with regular puff pastry for turnovers.

Marshmallow & Yam Hand Pies

Yields: 4 Servings

Ingredients:

1 crescent dough sheet/homemade crust
1 can (16 oz.) candied yams
1/2 t. cinnamon
1/4 t. of each:
-Allspice
-Salt
2 tbsp. marshmallow crème
1 egg

Ingredients for the Maple Glaze:

1/2 cup each:
-Confectioners' sugar
-Maple syrup

How to Prepare:

1. Program the heat setting on the AF to 400°F.
2. Drain the syrup from the yams. Combine the cinnamon, salt, allspice, and yams using a fork to the blend the spices and mash the yams.
3. Put the dough sheet onto a board and cut into four equal sections.
4. Spoon the filling onto the squares and add a tablespoon of the crème.
5. Use a brush to spread the egg over the edges of the dough and place the remainder of the two pieces of dough on top of the pies.

6. Use a fork to crimp the edges and cut three slits in the top for venting.
7. Place in the Air Fryer for six minutes.
8. Make the glaze from the sugar and syrup in a small dish—slowly adding the syrup—until the sugar dissolves.
9. To serve, drizzle the glaze over the warm pies and enjoy.

Orange & Pineapple Fondant

Yields: 4 Servings

Ingredients:

4.2 oz. each:
-Butter
-Dark chocolate
2 med. eggs
4 tbsp. castor sugar (see recipe below)
2 tbsp. self-rising flour
1 med. orange (rind and juice)

How to Prepare:

1. Grease four ramekins with a small amount of oil or cooking spray.
2. Program the heat in the Air Fryer to 356°F.
3. Cut and tear apart the orange and grate the orange peel.
4. Melt the butter and chocolate in a double boiler or a glass measuring cup over a pot of hot water. Stir until it is creamy smooth.
5. Beat and whisk in the sugar and eggs—until frothy and pale. Blend in the sugar and egg mixture along with the orange bits. Add the flour and mix until well blended.
6. Fill the ramekins about ¾ of the way full with the mixture. Cook in the Air Fryer for 12 minutes.
7. Take it from the fryer and let them rest for two minutes. (They will continue to cook.) Turn them out of the containers (upside down) into a serving platter. You can loosen the edges by tapping the ramekin gently with a butter knife.

8. The fondant will release from the center to provide you with a sweet center of pudding.
9. Garnish with some caramel sauce or vanilla ice cream.

Castor Sugar

Castor or caster sugar is merely granulated sugar that has been placed into a blender or food processor. Castor sugar is a fine sugar used for some recipes because it melts easier than regular sugar.

How to Prepare:

1. Put the granulated sugar into the blender/food processor.
2. Pulse until it is a 'super-fine' texture—not powdery.

Shortbread Fingers

Yields: 10 Servings

Ingredients:

2 c. all-purpose flour
¾ c. butter
1/3 c. castor sugar

How to Prepare:

1. Set the Air Fryer temperature to 356°F.
2. Combine the sugar and flour in a mixing container. Blend in the butter and knead until it is smooth.
3. Make the dough into finger cookie shapes and stab with a fork for the indentions.
4. Cook in the fryer on a baking sheet for 12 minutes.
5. *Note:* Preparation time is only four minutes with a 12-minute cooking time. If you like a firmer cookie, you can go for 14 minutes or even less time of ten minutes if you really want it soft.

Strawberry Cupcakes with Strawberry Icing

Yields: 10 Servings

Ingredients:

2 medium eggs
½ cup of each:
-Castor sugar
-Self-rising flour
-Icing sugar
1 c. butter - divided
½ t. vanilla essence
1 tbsp. whipped cream
½ t. pink food coloring
¼ c. fresh (blended) strawberries

How to Prepare:

1. Set the Air Fryer temperature to 338°F.
2. Cream 1/2 of the butter and sugar in a sizable mixing container until it is creamy smooth. Break the eggs into the mix one at a time along with the vanilla essence.
3. Blend in a small amount of flour at a time until all is thoroughly mixed.
4. Pour them into ramekins about 75% of the way full. Place them in the Air Fryer for eight minutes.
5. *Prepare the Frosting:* Cream the rest of the butter (1/2 cup) butter and slowly mix in the icing sugar until creamy. Pour in the food coloring (blended) strawberries, and whipped cream—mix well.
6. Take them out and use a piping bag to make the swirly frosting for a tasty cupcake every time.

Sweet Bacon Cookies

Yields: 6 Servings

Ingredients:

5 tbsp. keto-friendly peanut butter
4 slices cooked – chopped bacon
3 tbsp. swerve
¼ t. of each:
 -Ground ginger
 -Baking soda
½ t. vanilla extract

How to Prepare:

1. Warm up the Air Fryer to 350°F.
2. Combine all of the fixings – bacon last – in a large mixing bowl.
3. Once it is consistent – make it into a log. Break it apart into six segments. Roll the balls and gently flatten.
4. Arrange the cookies in the fryer basket and prepare for 7 minutes.
5. Chill when done and enjoy.

Bonus Recipe

By the Way, do you have a puppy? If so, you don't need to leave them out! Try this healthy treat for them:

Puppy Poppers

Ingredients:

1 c. peanut butter
½ c. unsweetened applesauce
1 t. baking powder
1 c. flour
2 c. oats

How to Prepare:

1. Mix the peanut butter and applesauce in a bowl until creamy.
2. Toss in the oats, baking powder, and flour. When smooth, roll out the dough into teaspoon sized balls.
3. Prepare the Air Fryer to reach 350°F.
4. Coat the bottom/bucket of the fryer basket with a little oil.
5. Arrange 8-12 of the balls in the basket and cook for eight minutes. Turn halfway through. Continue with the process with the batter until all are done. Cool completely before storing.
6. The poppers will stay fresh for up to two weeks.

Conclusion

Thanks for reading your entire copy of *The Air Fryer Bible: Complete Cookbook of Super Easy Recipes for Everyday Meals*. Let's hope it was informative and provided you with all of the tools you need to achieve your goals of preparing healthier meals for you and your family.

There are plenty of books offered on this subject in today's market, thanks again for choosing this one! Every effort was made to ensure that it is full of as much useful information as possible.

Finally, if you found this book useful in any way, a review is always appreciated!

Index for the Recipes

Chapter 2: Breakfast & Brunch Recipes

Chapter 3: Tasty Poultry Choices

9. Chinese Chicken Wings
10. Country-Style Chicken Tenders
11. Fried Chicken
12. Jamaican Chicken Meatballs
13. Lemon & Rosemary Chicken
14. Old Bay Chicken Wings
15. Orange Chicken Wings
16. Tarragon Chicken
17. Whole Chicken: Rotisserie Style

Turkey Specialties

1. Avocado & Turkey Burrito
2. Mozzarella Turkey Rolls
3. Roast Turkey Breast
4. Roast Turkey Reuben
5. Turkey Breast with Maple Mustard Glaze

Chapter 4: Beef Specialties

1. Beef Roll-Ups
2. Beef Stew
3. Country Fried Steak
4. Rib Steak
5. Roast Beef for Lunchtime Sandwiches
6. Spicy Shredded Beef
7. The Steak Rub
8. Steak – Medium-Rare

Ground Beef Choices

1. Beef & Bacon Taco Rolls
2. Beef & Potatoes
3. Beef Empanadas

4. Beef Schnitzel
5. Cheeseburgers Inside Out
6. Cheeseburger Mini Sliders
7. Cheeseburger Patties
8. Maggi Hamburgers
9. Meatloaf with Black Peppercorns
10. Taco Fried Egg Rolls

Chapter 5: Pork & Fish Choices

Pork Favorites

1. Bacon-Wrapped Pork Tenderloin
2. Crispy Breaded Pork Chops
3. Raspberry Balsamic Smoked Pork Chops
4. Roast Pork Loin with Red Potatoes
5. Southern Fried Pork Chops

Fish & Seafood

1. Breaded Fried Shrimp
2. Cajun Salmon
3. Cajun Shrimp
4. Catfish
5. Clams Oregano
6. Coconut Shrimp
7. Cod Steaks with Ginger
8. Cod Sticks
9. Crumbled Fish
10. Dill Salmon
11. Fish & Chips
12. Fish Tacos
13. Grilled Prawns/Shrimp
14. Halibut Steak with a Teriyaki Glazed Sauce
15. Lemon Fish

16. Salmon Croquettes
17. Salmon Patties

Chapter 6: Other Tasty Meats – Sides & Veggies

Variety Meals

1. Hot Dogs
2. Stromboli

Lamb

1. Lamb Meatballs
2. Roasted Rack of Lamb with a Macadamia Crust

Veggies

1. Avocado Fries
2. Avocado Bacon Fries
3. Baked Potatoes
4. Blossoming Onion
5. Broccoli
6. Brussels Sprouts
7. Buffalo Cauliflower
8. Button Mushroom Melt
9. Cauliflower Rice
10. Charred Shishito Peppers
11. Garlic & Thyme Tomatoes
12. Grilled Corn
13. Grilled Tomatoes
14. Honey Roasted Carrots
15. Mediterranean Veggies
16. Onion Rings
17. Parmesan Truffle Oil Fries

18. Potato Hash
19. Roasted Veggie Pasta Salad
20. Skinny Fries
21. Stuffed Mushrooms
22. Twice Baked Loaded Air-Fried Potatoes

Sides

Bread Choices

1. Bread Rolls with Potato Stuffing
2. Buttermilk Biscuits
3. Cheesy Garlic Bread
4. Garlic Knots
5. Phyllo Pastry

Chapter 7: Snacks & Appetizers

1. Apple Chips
2. Bacon-Wrapped Chicken
3. Bacon-Wrapped Prawns
4. Bacon-Wrapped Tater Tots
5. Cajun Spiced Snack Mix
6. Cheese Balls
7. Cheese & Onion Nuggets
8. Chickpeas with Ranch Seasoning
9. Crispy Corn Tortilla Chips
10. Feta Triangles
11. Fried Pickles
12. Garlic Roasted Almonds
13. Grilled Cheese Sandwich
14. Kale Chips
15. Mac "N" Cheese Balls
16. Mini Bacon Wrapped Burritos – Vegan

17. Mini Quiche Wedges
18. Mozzarella Sticks
19. Party Meatballs
20. Pigs in A Blanket
21. Pita Bread Cheese Pizza
22. Potato Skin Wedges
23. Spiced Nuts
24. Sweet & Salty Snack Mix
25. Zucchini Roll-Ups

Chapter 8: Desserts

1. Air Fried Plantains
2. Apple Fries with Caramel Cream Dip
3. Apricot & Blackberry Crumble
4. Blackberry Pie
5. Cheesecake
6. Cherry Pie
7. Chocolate Chip Cookies
8. Chocolate Soufflés
9. Donut Bread Pudding
10. Green Avocado Pudding
11. Lemon Ricotta Cheesecake
12. Marshmallow Peanut Butter Turnovers
13. Marshmallow & Yam Hand Pies
14. Orange & Pineapple Fondant
15. How to Make Castor Sugar
16. Shortbread Fingers
17. Strawberry Cupcakes with Strawberry Icing
18. Sweet Bacon Cookies

CPSIA information can be obtained
at www.ICGtesting.com
Printed in the USA
BVHW07s0102141018
530042BV00001B/1/P

9 781719 889711